Praise for *The Spirit of O*

"This is a fascinating book by a remarkable man. Jim
excitement and power of entrepreneurship can cha
made that happen in our community and communities throughout South Carolina. For
many of our young people, lessons learned about entrepreneurship can be one of the most
important educational experiences of their lives. This book is proof of that."

Joseph P. Riley, Jr., Mayor
City of Charleston, South Carolina

"YEScarolina perfectly embodies the notion that entrepreneurial education is paramount
to solving the problem of poverty. By nurturing the natural talents and attitudes of low
income youth, YEScarolina gives kids the tools to transform street smarts into business
smarts."

Steve Mariotti, Founder
Network for Teaching Entrepreneurship

"Jimmy Bailey's passion for YEScarolina is palpable—in person and in print. YEScarolina is not only a great South Carolina story, but a heartwarming, American story."

Walter Edgar, Radio Host
"Walter Edgar's Journal" on ETV-SC

"These kids have mastered the critical skill of turning challenges into opportunities, which
is just as valuable off the court as it is on."

Pat Williams, Senior VP
NBA's Orlando Magic

"For teachers everywhere who have asked themselves 'What is it all for?' here is the answer.
These stories are a reminder that we CAN make a difference in the lives of our students.
YEScarolina plants the seeds of youth entrepreneurship into the fertile minds of students
across South Carolina."

Paul Smith Jr. MBA, Assistant Professor of Business
Newberry College

"*The Spirit of Outreach* is a wonderful tribute to the memory of Mark Motley. These
stories are an inspiration for educational professionals everywhere."

Aimee R. Gray, Certified Entrepreneurship Teacher

THE SPIRIT OF OUTREACH

INSPIRING STORIES *from YEScarolina*
and the Mark Elliott Motley Foundation

THE SPIRIT OF
OUTREACH

*INSPIRING STORIES from YEScarolina
and the Mark Elliott Motley Foundation*

COMPILED BY JIMMY BAILEY

FOREWORD BY RONALD L. MOTLEY

Advantage®

Published by Advantage, Charleston, South Carolina.
Member of Advantage Media Group.

ADVANTAGE is a registered trademark and the Advantage colophon is a trademark of Advantage Media Group, Inc.

Printed in the United States of America.

ISBN: 978-1-59932-177-6
LCCN: 2010911818

This publication is designed to provide accurate and authoritative information in regard to the subject matter covered. It is sold with the understanding that the publisher is not engaged in rendering legal, accounting, or other professional services. If legal advice or other expert assistance is required, the services of a competent professional person should be sought.

Advantage Media Group is proud to be a part of the Tree Neutral® program. Tree Neutral offsets the number of trees consumed in the production and printing of this book by taking proactive steps such as planting trees in direct proportion to the number of trees used to print books. To learn more about Tree Neutral, please visit www.treeneutral.com. To learn more about Advantage's commitment to being a responsible steward of the environment, please visit www.advantagefamily.com/green

Advantage Media Group is a publisher of business, self-improvement, and professional development books and online learning. We help entrepreneurs, business leaders, and professionals share their Stories, Passion, and Knowledge to help others Learn & Grow. Do you have a manuscript or book idea that you would like us to consider for publishing? Please visit advantagefamily.com or call 1.866.775.1696.

In loving memory of

Mark Elliott Motley

JULY 15, 1972 – FEBRUARY 13, 2000

My son Mark was a young man of extraordinary courage. At the age of 27, he was dedicated to the mission of self-betterment through a painful medical procedure, one to hopefully better control his epilepsy. I realized what a remarkable man he had become when he tackled his epilepsy so strongly and bravely, though it ultimately cost him his life. I felt such love and pride in him, and deep awe at the courage he displayed. Mark was gentle but strong, kind, generous. He was deeply loyal and always the first to forgive. He kept our family focused on the simple but important things in life and he led our family through many happy times and through rough waters in his very quiet, unassuming way. He so loved his family, his friends, the sea – enjoying the water and the sky – and the music of Jimmy Buffet. His courage and strength are a tribute to us all and he is never far from my mind nor from my heart.

– RONALD L. MOTLEY

FOREWORD

RONALD L. MOTLEY, ESQ.
Chairman and Director
The Mark Elliott Motley Foundation

If my son Mark were here to read this book, he would be proud of each and every one of these young entrepreneurs who are proving to the world and to themselves that they will make it. In his twenty-eight years on this earth, Mark touched many others with his caring spirit, and he particularly enjoyed working with young people.

In 2002, I established the Mark Elliott Motley Foundation, dedicated to improving the lives of children and young adults. We are proud to be one of YEScarolina's major benefactors. As it nurtures entrepreneurs, YEScarolina exemplifies my son's desire to help others. He yearned to better the world for those to whom life had dealt difficulties.

Mark experienced firsthand, in his own family, the spirit of outreach. When Mark was a young boy, our family took in a child who was in need. Throughout Mark's short life, he considered him to be one of his best friends, and I am grateful to have had the opportunity to see that young person through college. Another friend of Mark's came into his life in college, and we reached out to him, helping him through his college years. He now works at my law firm as a partner.

I am grateful as well that my career has enabled me to reach out to victims of destructive power. We have tackled the asbestos and tobacco industries. We are helping survivors and family members of those who perished in the 9/11 terrorist attacks find justice against those who financed that atrocity.

It was always Mark's nature to help others, volunteering in an orphanage and wherever else he found the need for a kind heart and encouraging smile. His own particular challenge was epilepsy, and his condition was steadily worsening. He diligently researched different treatments and decided to go to one of the country's leading hospitals for brain surgery, hoping that the outcome would give him a chance at a normal life. His high hopes, however, went tragically wrong – he died of complications two days after the procedure.

My son's gift was compassion, and the foundation that now bears his name seeks out organizations that likewise show, through their caring for and giving to young people, that they are worthy of our financial support. Such is the spirit of YEScarolina as it reaches out and lifts up the youth of South Carolina by teaching them how to prosper in difficult times, even when life has dealt them challenges that can seem insurmountable.

Nearly a decade after his passing, Mark Elliott Motley is still giving.

Sincerely,
RONALD L. MOTLEY

CREAM OF THE CROP

T hey come from across the great state of South Carolina – its plateaus and mountains, its midlands and coastal plain. The young men and women you will meet in the following pages have defied the odds. They are giving life their best shot as they become the business leaders of tomorrow, pursuing their fortunes and their passions.

They range in age from 13 to 20, some just starting middle school, a few already embarking on college. You will meet landscapers and bakers, writers and artisans, hairdressers and fashion designers and more. Half are young men, half are young women; some have established their businesses, and the rest are well on their way.

All express gratitude to a program that has put South Carolina in the forefront among states encouraging such young enterprise. It's called Youth Entrepreneurship South Carolina (or YEScarolina, for short). The program certifies teachers in schools across the state to help their students launch business ideas, and these students are a sampling of the talent that might otherwise have gone untapped.

Each of those profiled here has been recognized by his or her school or community as an entrepreneurial student of the year – which means that each represents numerous other industrious youth, all worthy of recognition. Many of the hundreds that YEScarolina has helped come from humble homes – and early struggles engender a fortitude that spells business success. Such souls are creative. They are accustomed to stress. They are unafraid of failure.

Hear their own words: "Go for your dreams." "Be persistent." "Learn from your mistakes." "Believe in yourself." "Don't let people talk you down." "Stay in school." "Don't stop." Over and over, as you will see, they urge their peers to forge ahead and demand more from life.

And they tell how their attitudes and goals changed under the tutelage of entrepreneurship teachers in public schools trained by YEScarolina – over seven hundred, so far, more than any other state. Beginning in 2004, the program also has been running college-based summer camps. They quickly tripled from the initial seven. The current goal is to run forty-six, one for each county – and perhaps twice that many in the years ahead as YEScarolina pursues further avenues of private and government funding. The students get a chance to compete against students across the country through the Network for Teaching Entrepreneurship.

YEScarolina has earned national recognition, as well. In 2009, the city of Charleston won a first-place livability award from the U.S. Conference of Mayors: Youth who were trained by YEScarolina learned to turn their street smarts into business smarts. They had been peddling roses they made from palmetto fronds, and though some merchants had considered the youngsters a nuisance, the program assured them their ingenuity was welcome – and, through training, they channeled their energy into an asset to tourism. To be recognized by the nation's mayors is a high honor: Mayors get it. They are on the front lines in the battle for social change, and they see firsthand the life-related skills our youth so badly need.

Here then, in alphabetical order, are some of South Carolina's finest.

TALENTED YOUTH ENTREPRENEURS

ANDREW AIKMAN, 17, Sullivan's Island, mobile automobile detailing

KIMBERLY M. ANDERSON, 19, Mayesville, teen magazine editor

VICTORIA OLABUNMI BAILEY, 13, Columbia, photographer

RICHARD BLACK, 14, Blythewood, novelty shop owner

CHANDLER BOLT, 19, Charleston, landscaping, house painting

SABLE BOWLER, 17, Irmo, specialty fashion shoes

AQUILA O. BROWN, 16, Charleston, hand-drawn portrait service

DAMIEN BROWN, 16, Charleston, palmetto rose artisan

RACHAEL BROWN, 13, Orangeburg, baker

TOMMY BROWN, 15, Rock Hill, landscaper

SYDNEY JOHANNA BRYANT, 13, Iva, hair bow designer

HUNTER DEAN, 17, Beaufort, biofuels dealer

ELYSE DELGADO, 17, Charleston, cookbook publisher

HILLMAN GARRETT DORN, 18, Edgefield County, roof and gutter serviceman

ESSENCE EADDY, 20, Marion, day spa operator

ZAKIRA D. FELDER, 12, Gresham, child care provider

TYLER FREEMAN, 16, Isle of Palms, cornhole game board maker

DETRIA L. GRAHAM, 18, Florence, photographer

MAGGIE GRISELL, 16, Greenville, cookie baker

TRAVIS GROSE, 12, North Augusta, lawn care

JOHN JENKINS, 17, Dalzell, men's jewelry and accessories salesman

EVAN KNOX, 16, Johns Island, website and graphic design

SHANNON LARIBO, 16, Ladson, writers' site webmaster

KRISTEN LINSCOTT, 17, Mount Pleasant, candle design business

JOSEPH LONG, 15, Anderson, retail apparel business

BRYANNA MCCAIN, 17, Edgefield County, youth tutor

JESUS OLJUJUAN CHRISTOPHER "CHRIS" MCCREARY, 18, Rock Hill, barber

TAKISHA MCCULLOUGH, 18, Charleston, graphic designer

DENISHA MCDUFFIE, 17, Sumter, hair salon operator

MANDY MCGILL, 18, Starr, custom-made christian t-shirts

MARIELLE MCLAURIN, 19, Charleston, face painter

KAREN MOK, 18, North Charleston, greeting card writer and designer

WALLACE MOORE, 16, Marion, computer web service

JOHNNY MORGAN OWEN, 13, Hamer, cookie company owner

JALON PERCY, 14, Columbia, business graphic designer

CLARA PILLEY, 12, Charleston, non-profit—Keys for Hope

TYLER SHAW PINCKNEY, 17, Charleston, graphic design

KESHA RAINEY, 18, Charleston, pearl jewelry collection

ASHLEY LAUREN SEASE, 16, Irmo, fashion designer

CATHERINE ELIZABETH HENRIAN SHOWS, 16, Summerville, fashion accessory designer

NICK SISK, 17, Charleston, diesel apparel

JEROME SMALLS, 14, North Charleston, handyman

EMMA-GRACE SPACH, 12, Mount Pleasant, non-profit—Keys for Hope

MICKEY J. SUBER, 18, Newberry, photo package designer

NICK VAN DER TOORN, 17, Walhalla, eBay consigner

AIDYN TRUBEY, 12, Charleston, fishing magazine publisher

VICTORIA TURNER, 15, Summerville, photography service

LUKE VARADI, 17, Charleston, fishing charter business

SHANE WHITEHEAD, 14, Columbia, landscaper

MARCUS WILLIAMS, 16, Charleston, author

ERIN WILLIS, 17, Charleston, reselling on consignment

M. GRACE YOUNGBLOOD, 15, Columbia, jewelry designer

ADAM ZERBST, 17, Charleston, healthy snack foods

Andrew Aikman

Mobile Automobile Detailing

"It is best to act upon a good idea as soon as possible."

Age: 17

Community: Sullivan's Island

Wando High School

Teacher: Mrs. Misty Rohaly

A ndrew's plan for the future is anchored in his interest in cars. He recognizes that car detailing requires a specific skill set and that he needs to act on his ideas swiftly to make a profit.

When did you first hear about YEScarolina?

During my first week in my entrepreneurship class, our teacher, Misty Rohaly, told us about YEScarolina and the business plan competition. When I first heard about it, I thought the competition sounded quite interesting, and I was excited to compete in it.

I am very interested in cars, so I made my plan for an automobile detailing business. Detailing a vehicle properly takes a certain skill and a knack for perfection. The business plan that I made for the competition was just for an example of what mine would look like if I worked in my business full time.

What's the hardest lesson you've learned?

I have not yet set up "Drew's Detailing," although I have occasionally detailed people's cars for profit. Many of my lessons are still to come, but one thing I can say is that it is best to act upon a good idea as soon as possible. I started detailing cars two years ago, and I wish I had turned my occasional source of pocket change into a real company. That would have been a much more educational work experience than I have had in the three jobs I have worked since.

What do you plan to be doing five years from now?

YEScarolina, the mentors, and my teachers have taught me so much about entrepreneurship in the last few months. I plan to take this experience with me for the rest of my life, and utilize it in starting my own business or businesses in the future. The generosity of all of those who are involved in YEScarolina has inspired me to give back to the community when I become successful. When I am able to, I plan to give donations to organizations such as YEScarolina that help the community by mentoring students to become entrepreneurs.

Kimberly M. Anderson

Teen Magazine Editor

"Sometimes, I catch myself writing something I never knew I had in me. This makes me think of all the emotions that others have built up inside of them and try to get out."

Age: 19
Community: Mayesville
Crestwood High School
Teacher: Ms. Linda Avery

A monthly magazine focusing on the talents of Sumter County area teens, written for them and by them, is Kimberly M. Anderson's entrepreneurial enterprise. Through stories, artwork, poetry and more, Kimberly says, contributors can "show others what they are truly made of, and it gives them the freedom to express themselves openly" without having to conform to society's norms.

When did you hear about YEScarolina?

I heard about the program when I was 17, and I came up with my idea for my business when I was a senior in high school. My business entrepreneur teacher, Mrs. Linda Avery, was my coach throughout the whole affair, and when she got me involved with YEScarolina, they gave me an even bigger push.

What is your typical day like, and how do you do your work?

After my college classes are over for the day, I work on school-related activities or on the concept of the magazine. I am also involved in two clubs: SIFE (Students in Free Enterprise) and AAS (African American Society). My day is filled with many things.

My life is a book. I love to write to encourage and uplift. Sometimes, I catch myself writing something I never knew I had in me. This makes me think of all the emotions that others have built up inside of them and try to get out. The work I get out of them I use to uplift others or open a broader horizon. My work is natural. I don't want anything I publish to be forced; I want it to be real and authentic.

How would your best friend describe what you're doing?

My best friend often describes me by saying "this young lady is an old lady," because of the old spirit I possess. "She doesn't mind putting herself out there to help someone else," states Latisha King. Others have told me this as well.

What's the hardest lesson you've learned?

It's hard to get kids to express themselves openly. Sometimes it comes down to sharing your own experiences in order to get them to share theirs. I've found that I sometimes feel uneasy sharing my personal life with someone I hardly know. However, I'm slowly but surely getting over my shyness and becoming more open to strangers.

What has been your biggest surprise?

I was welcomed back to New York for the second time in order to attend the NFTE (Network for Teaching Entrepreneurship) business plan school. It was very nice. They paid for everything, and I got a free laptop. This most influential experience taught me more about the business, and I met other young entrepreneurs. It feels nice being able to network in places other than South Carolina.

What has been your biggest break?

I was contacted by an investor who was interested in my business proposal. I also got invited to travel the world with the international scholar laureate. There are a lot of things that I'm being accepted into in order to help better my business. These opportunities are making me well known and are allowing others to become more acquainted with my business. It's all about putting my name out there.

What would you tell somebody else interested in business?

As long as you have the perseverance to push for more, I encourage you to do so. It takes a lot of work and energy to run, let alone create, your own business. Also, make sure that you have a relationship with God. You will be looked upon as a role model. So, you must be prepared to fight and win.

What do you expect to be doing five years from now?

I plan to have started my business and attend graduate school. Also, I will be in the process of writing plays. I love Tyler Perry – he is an inspiration through laughter, and I always love making people smile.

So, with that, I would like to propose another business plan. I want to open an art theater for young kids who like to act but cannot afford it. I plan to be very busy throughout the next five years.

Victoria Olabunmi Bailey

Photographer

"A good business plan can be turned into a profitable business."

Age: 13
Community: Columbia
Engenuity Biz Camp
Teacher: Mr. Paul Smith

The wonders of our world, whether the beauty of nature or the smile of a child, are worth preserving for all time, and Victoria Olabunmi Bailey knows how. Her entrepreneurial idea: a photography business. Her focus, she says, would be "on the kids, to capture the memories of their lives." Her dreams are big, and she says she's still waiting for her big break.

What is your typical day like, and how do you do your work?

On a typical day, I wake up early for school. Then after school, I start on my homework and study for upcoming exams. After that's done, I'll watch TV and talk to my friends. My business plan involves recommending the scenery for my clients, listening to their vision of what they want to do, coming up with a time to do the photo shoot, and taking the pictures and printing them.

How would your best friend describe what you're doing?

My best friend would say that I am a tinier version of a business-woman. She always knew that I would do something so professional.

What's the hardest lesson you've learned?

The hardest lesson would be to establish a good business. Since I'm not finished with my education, it is hard to understand the financial parts.

What has been your biggest surprise?

The biggest surprise so far is that I have a good business plan that can be turned into a profitable business.

What would you tell somebody else interested in business?

What I would say to somebody who wanted to do a photography business would be to be organized because it is very easy to get work mixed up.

What do you expect to be doing five years from now?

In five years, I will be 18 years old and a freshman in college.

Richard Black

Novelty Shop Owner

"When I make a sale, I am careful to package the product nicely, make it available to the customer as soon as possible, and follow up to see if everything was done to satisfaction."

Age: 14

Community: Blythewood

Dent Middle School Biz Camp

Teacher: Ms. Joyce Simons

At his school's 13th annual Black Expo, Richard Black was displaying his artwork when the YEScarolina teacher stopped to take a look and told him about the program's business camp opportunities. That launched his idea for a novelty shop to sell his art – and his mother has long saved most all his creative endeavors. He calls his business Ribbons and Bows Inc., with the slogan "Something for Everyone" – including T-shirts, trivets, and toys he designed.

What is your typical day like, and how do you do your work?

I am a typical middle school student who starts my day living my life and getting ready for my future. By the time I get to high school, I will have four of my freshman credits completed. Art is always at my fingertips, whether I'm preparing a new product for my business or just completing a school assignment. My business operates out of a department store downtown. I have sample items on display. Other vendors have their items on display as well. I sit at my location and greet passersby. I share my art items with them and have business cards ready to hand out. I always have items ready to sell, or orders can be placed. This location gives me very good exposure as a young entrepreneur. I also use word of mouth and contacts with friends and family to advertise my business. I use brochures, a PowerPoint, and free samples to attract buyers. When I make a sale, I am careful to package the product nicely, make it available to the customer as soon as possible, and follow up to see if everything was done to satisfaction.

I spend a lot of time coming up with new and varied products for my novelty shop. Whether I'm focused on my business or any other aspect of my life, I am always forward thinking.

How would your best friend describe what you're doing?

My best friend would describe what I'm doing as "taking care of business," literally! He sees my art ability as an asset and thinks that I could someday make great album covers.

What's the hardest lesson you've learned?

Since my business deals with art items, the original is valued more than the copy. It is challenging for me to give up the original item. With my drawings, paintings, and comic books, it is easy to make prints. Although I have more than one of some items, each item is an original. Overall, the hardest lesson that I've had so far is that sometimes I don't succeed in making a sale. Beauty is in the eyes of the beholder, and not everyone will find all of my products as appealing as my mom or I do.

What has been your biggest surprise?

I came in third place at Biz Camp at my school. There were a lot of students competing and many of them had humanitarian and goodwill business proposals. My business was more about aesthetics, and I wasn't sure how I would place. But, in the end, I knew that art was a universal language that could speak to the hearts and souls of all people.

What has been your biggest break?

My lifelong goal is to become a doctor. My mom tells me I might draw my way through medical school. After participating in some "shadowing experiences" in the field, I knew I had the passion to become a doctor, but I've learned how expensive it is to become one. I think Ribbons and Bows Inc. has set me on a path to success.

I want to thank my brother for letting me help him raise money when he wanted to enter the Soapbox Derby when I was in second grade. We wrote and sold a lot of books outside of school and in our neighborhood. We learned a great deal about patience and perseverance, and set an obtainable goal of raising the $50 entry fee. Years later, I entered the Soapbox Derby and won a savings bond.

My mom was my Stock Market Game coach when I was in elementary school. Perhaps being on the team set me on the path to entrepreneurship. She also saved my artwork, and now I have a nice collection. I have improved through participation in activities at the South Carolina Art Museum and in the Tri-DAC Art Consortium in my school district.

What would you tell somebody else interested in business?
It could present a huge opportunity for them. It is a great way to learn things about businesses and careers. They could also find out a lot about themselves and the direction they want to pursue in life.

What do you expect to be doing five years from now?
Hopefully I'll be attending college and studying something that will help to enrich the lives of other people.

Chandler Bolt

Landscaping, House Painting

"I'd like to launch a public speaking business so that I can travel the U.S. motivating others and inspiring the next generation of entrepreneurs."

Age: 19

Community: Charleston

Walhalla High School, College of Charleston

Teacher: Mrs. Harriet Templin

Chandler Bolt's lawn care service grew into a house-painting business that did $100,000 in business over a summer. He and his brother are writing a book to share the lessons their parents taught them.

When did you first hear about YEScarolina?

I first heard about YEScarolina when I was 16 years old. I heard about it through my high school entrepreneurship teacher who was certified by Jimmy Bailey to teach entrepreneurship. I wrote my business plan for my first business in my entrepreneurship class.

I ran a landscaping, lawn care and pressure washing business before college and was able to make some good money to put toward college expenses. Running this business opened up the opportunity to run a house painting business the following summer. I worked really hard at this and was able to run over $100,000 in business while painting and pressure washing over 40 houses in low country South Carolina. From this hard work, I also earned the title of national "Entrepreneur of the Year" within the Student Painters organization.

I owe all this to YEScarolina, Jimmy Bailey, and my entrepreneurship teacher Mrs. Harriet Templin. Because of them, I was able to start my first two small businesses, and those businesses gave me the confidence to continue reaching higher.

What is your typical day like, and how do you do your work?

When running my painting business, I did most of my sales and marketing during the spring. My business was based out of Summerville (where my brother lives), and I would go there every weekend to do marketing and estimates with homeowners. I hired five college students to work full time painting houses during the summer. It was awesome to be able to help other students pay for their college tuition.

This year, I'm helping mentor a group of college students from College of Charleston. They'll be able to run a business just like I did and get an amazing experience in the process. I hope that I can give them the learning experience that I was given, because it completely changed my life.

What does being an entrepreneur mean to you?

Being an entrepreneur is a thrilling experience, but it's a roller coaster ride. There are plenty of ups and downs along the way. The hardest lesson for me to learn has been that there's no such thing as a failure.

When I first started, I let small failures get to me, and they really wore me down. As bad as it feels to fail at something, I finally realized that all failures are opportunities for growth. My biggest successes have always come after a brief period of "failure." It's much easier to push through periods of "failure" when you know that success is waiting on the other side.

What has been your biggest surprise?

I've been really surprised by how eager people are to help. Since starting, I've received amazing advice and encouragement from so many people. Local newspapers and TV stations have done stories on my business and, even local mayors Keith Summey and Joe Riley have reached out to show their support. I never would have thought this would happen!

What would you tell somebody else interested in business?

Do it! It's such an amazing experience and you'll learn so much in the process. This program has changed my life forever, and I'm so glad that I started my first small business through YEScarolina.

Once you catch the entrepreneurship bug, it's hard to imagine doing anything else. It's so much fun to be able to run a business and create something for yourself. Even if you're intimidated by the notion of running your own business, you can start small to gain confidence. It will pay off.

What do you expect to be doing five years from now?

This spring I'll be releasing a book that I co-authored with my brother titled Breaking out of a Broken System. The book shares the lessons our parents taught us over many years that many people never get the chance to learn. All of the profit goes to local charities Palmetto Medical Initiative and YEScarolina.

In the next five years, I hope to launch my own company on a much larger scale. The two areas I'm interested in are real estate and software as a service. I'd like to launch a public speaking business so that I can travel the U.S. motivating others and inspiring the next generation of entrepreneurs.

Sable Bowler

Specialty Fashion Shoes

"Be dedicated. Make sure that this is something that you really want to do, because this is a lot of work and requires your full attention."

Age: 17
Community: Irmo
Dutch Fork High School
Teacher: Ms. Norma Brown

S able Bowler has her own take on the old expression "If the shoe fits, wear it" – and that is, "For shoes that fit, start a business." Her fashion line caters to "Unique Soles" who need larger sizes.

When did you first hear about YEScarolina?

I was invited to my first business plan competition at the age of 17 in Charleston. The name of my business is Unique Soles. This is a specialty store that caters to women with bigger-size feet. I start from size 11-14. I started my idea because my dad wore a size 18 shoe. I inherited his genes, wearing a size 13 shoe. I get aggravated when shopping for shoes because I can never find fashionable shoes to wear, I can only find sneakers, so I decided to solve a problem not only for myself but for other women struggling with this issue. After researching my market, I found that there are not a lot of stores that carry bigger-size shoes. I realized that there is a great demand for Unique Soles.

What is your typical day like, and how do you do your work?

Right now I buy from wholesalers online and sell my shoes on the Internet. Eventually I plan on designing my own shoes and having the "Unique Soles" name on my shoes. I also want to get my business up and running online and then open a physical store.

What's the hardest lesson you've learned?

The hardest lesson I've learned so far is basically managing school, work and my business. It sometimes gets very hectic, and at times I can't keep up. This is a learning experience, and I'm learning to manage everything as I go along.

What has been your biggest surprise?

My biggest surprise so far has been being invited to the 2013 inauguration. I got a chance to witness history first hand. I also met a lot of people from around the world. I met people from Africa, Saudi Arabia, California, and some who lived just a couple of miles from me but I didn't even know. I visited monuments like FDR and the Lincoln Memorial and the Martin Luther King monument. I also went to the inauguration ball. That just showed me that I can do anything!

What would you tell somebody else interested in business?

Be dedicated. Make sure that this is something that you really want to do, because this is a lot of work and requires your full attention.

What do you expect to be doing in five years from now?

In five years, I plan to have graduated from college with degrees in business, performing arts, and broadcast journalism. I also plan to be a very successful businesswoman. I plan to have a physical storefront location and to have customers all over the world (famous and all) buying shoes from me. I also plan to have my own shoes with my brand on them. Overall, I plan to be very successful and grounded.

Aquila O. Brown

Hand-Drawn Portrait Service

"Set your goals high, and do not let anyone tell you what you can and cannot do."

Age: 16

Community: Charleston

Charleston Charter School for Math and Science

Teacher: Ms. Micki Boulineau

Aquila offers outstanding customer service to the clientele of Trusol Art, her portrait service. She also recognizes the value in giving back to the community, either through education, volunteering or financial contribution.

When did you first hear about YEScarolina?

I first heard about YEScarolina in my business class. We were discussing the details of the business plan competition. My plan was for my business, Trusol Art, a hand-drawn portrait service created for individual preferences and memories.

What is a typical day like, and how do you do your work?

On a typical day, I draw portraits at home or out in the community. This means a lot to me because entrepreneurship is a form of loyalty that involves treating others with loving kindness. My way of staying true to myself is to provide outstanding customer service. That is a part of my character and who I am.

What's the hardest lesson you've learned?

The hardest thing I've learned in my business is to stay focused and be persistent. I am a sole proprietor, so sometimes I have a lot of pictures to draw. It can be very stressful at times because I want to make sure I get every detail right. Despite that stress, it is relaxing and therapeutic to see the portrait when it is finished and the outcome of my work. The customer's satisfaction makes it even better.

What has been your biggest surprise?

The biggest surprise I've come across so far in my business is its feasibility. So many people like this form of art. I have drawn in different places like churches, food courts, and parks, and it amazes me how people of all ages are so curious – especially little kids who would say, "Can you draw me pleeassse?"

What would you tell somebody else interested in business?

To anyone who is interested in starting a business, my word of advice is to go in with a focused plan. Set your goals high, and do not let anyone tell you what you can and cannot do. People are interested in all kinds of things, especially new ideas. If someone tells you not to bother, move on. There are over seven billion people in the world and I promise you everyone is not going to say the same thing. That means you have a guaranteed "yes." Have confidence in everything you do, find your market, and you will make it! Failure is not falling; failure is when you don't get up and try again.

Most of all, do not forget to give back to your community. Trusol Art is planning to give back to the community by participating in community events, volunteering at places like the Children's

Museum, and helping children who have been sexually abused. We will also donate money to nonprofit organizations and charities such as Darkness to Light and my church.

Damien Brown

Palmetto Rose Craftsman

"Stay in school, and don't let anyone tell you that you can't succeed."

Age: 16
Community: Charleston
City of Charleston Biz Camp
Teacher: Ms. Jenny Whittle

Since he was seven years old, Damien Brown has been making and selling roses that he creates from palmetto fronds. "I first started selling them on the market in downtown Charleston," he says. By the time Damien was fourteen, he was taking business classes at the College of Charleston – and "now, I ship my roses across the world." He was introduced to YEScarolina when he was thirteen.

What is your typical day like, and how do you do your work?

I order all the stocks, start twisting them, and then I ship them out.

How would your best friend describe what you're doing?

My best friend would describe what I'm doing with my business as a grown man's job. I have an early start, so if I study business in college, I will be ahead.

What's the hardest lesson you've learned?

The hardest lesson I have ever learned so far is to never depend on anyone. It is also important to get an early start.

What has been your biggest surprise?

If you work very hard, it will pay off. Another surprise was when one lady ordered 225 roses for a wedding. The total cost of the roses was $675.

What would you tell somebody else interested in business?

I would tell someone else who wants to have a career like mine to stay in school, and don't let anyone tell you that you can't succeed.

What do you expect to be doing five years from now?

I would like to be in college doing sports and business. I will really pay attention to my classes, because doing well academically is a major boost in the career, and I want to succeed.

sponsored by:

Jimmy Bailey

Tommy Brown

Landscaper

"I do it right, I provide peace of mind, and I am thorough."

Age: 15
Community: Rock Hill
Rock Hill High School
Teacher: Ms. Jennifer Molnar

Tommy Brown is a professional at age 15, offering an array of landscaping services: "I mow, lawn trim, edge, fertilize, provide weed control, hedge trimming, and rake leaves." Other youths might earn some pocket money doing lawns, but Tommy is a cut above: He prides himself in the thoroughness of his work and the confidence he instills in his clients.

When did you hear about YEScarolina?

I first heard about YEScarolina when I was 15. Attending the business camp for YEScarolina at the College of Charleston was a huge honor, and I learned so much through this experience. The staff at YEScarolina was extremely supportive and provided resources and lessons that I can take with me through the rest of my life. It was also really cool that Jimmy Bailey came out to New York to watch and support me during the competition. I thank God and Jesus Christ that this opportunity was bestowed upon me. It was a lot of hard work!

What is your typical day like, and how do you do your work?

Since it is the fall and winter season, I go to school by bus, and then go to baseball practice. I participate in church and youth group functions on the weekends.

In my lawn and landscaping services, I do it right, I provide peace of mind, and I am thorough.

How would your best friend describe what you're doing?

I have a neighbor, who happens to be a really good friend of mine, who sees how I try to excel in everything I do – whether it's in school, sports, business, and as a person.

What's the hardest lesson you've learned?

I've had to learn how to balance my straight A average with sports, along with my commitment to my landscaping services.

What has been your biggest surprise?

I was on the front page of my local newspaper, *The Herald*. I received a congratulatory letter from the governor of South Carolina. My school principal announced this in front of the whole school!

What has been your biggest break?

I went to New York with my dad to compete in a national business competition. It was truly an opportunity of a lifetime that I will never forget.

What would you tell somebody else interested in business?

I would say to focus, work hard, pay attention, be patient, and have a solid short-term, as well as long-term, business plan.

What do you expect to be doing five years from now?

I will be a junior at a major university, hopefully on a full scholarship. I would like to study mechanical engineering.

Rachael Brown

Baker

"I often helped my grandmother make scratch biscuits. She is no longer with me on this earth, but I am keeping her spirit alive because most of my recipes are her old recipes."

Age: 13

Community: Orangeburg

Carver-Edisto Middle School

Teacher: Ms. Norma Rockwell

For special occasions, thirteen-year-old Rachael Brown bakes cakes and cookies for family members, and she intends to turn this pursuit into a livelihood. "My grandmother left her recipe box for me with all of her very old family recipes inside," she explains, and she has gathered recipes from others, as well. "Most of my customers are family and will order a cake or cookie from the family recipe box." She hears the same thing from each of them: After she finishes school, she should open a bakery. She heard about YEScarolina when she was 12.

What is your typical day like, and how do you do your work?

My typical baking day is usually for special occasions since I am still in school. Sometimes I can mix the cookie dough ahead of time and freeze it until the day before the party so that the cookies will be the most fresh. I also bake the cake about a day ahead so that my mom will have time to ice it.

Most people request the kind of dessert or cookie they would prefer. Then my mom drives me to the store to gather my ingredients. I have collected many shapes of pans for different shapes of cakes for different occasions.

How would your best friend describe what you're doing?

One of my friends described what I am doing as "delicious." She said that she is happy I am baking the family recipes because the adults are too busy and she misses my grandmother's cookies. My love of baking and cooking began early, as I often helped my grandmother make scratch biscuits around the age of five. Whatever she was cooking, she let me help. She is no longer with me on this earth, but I am keeping her spirit alive with my baking because most of my recipes are her old recipes.

What's the hardest lesson you've learned?

It is tiring standing in the kitchen with the oven to be sure the cookies do not bake too long or they will be too hard. If the cookies bake too long, then I have to start over, mixing and baking.

What has been your biggest surprise?

The biggest surprise I have had in my years of baking experience was the large number of people in my family who do not like to bake and are very happy that I do. I was also surprised that my little cousin wants to follow in my footsteps with baking.

What has been your biggest break?

My cousin asked me to bake the cake for my aunt's fiftieth wedding anniversary. My mom helped me with that one. We used a butter recipe cake batter and baked it into a half sheet cake. There were lots of people outside of my family that tasted my cake and really liked it. Some wrote my name and number down so that I can bake for them later.

What would you tell somebody else interested in business?

I love baking and what I would tell somebody else who wanted to do this is get lots of recipes and let lots of people taste your baking. The more people taste, the more customers you can have.

What do you expect to be doing five years from now?

I will be a high school senior in five years, and I would love to have my business built up to having a baking order every weekend. I want to create recipes of my own in a few years, but right now people love grandmother's, and I am happy to bake what the people want.

Sydney Johanna Bryant

Hair Bow Designer

"One thing I would like to do is involve some charitable organization with my business. It would be especially nice to donate bows to underprivileged little girls."

Age: 13

Community: Iva

YEScarolina Biz Camp, Anderson

Teacher: Ms. Aimee Gray

As a 13-year-old entrepreneur, Sydney Johanna Bryant already has learned to think out of the box , and "Out of the Box Bows" is what she calls her hair bow business. She chose the name because she uses a variety of products to make them. She designs some of them and makes others to order. "I have three younger sisters who love to wear bows in their hair," Sydney says. Recalling how hard it was to find just the right bow for an outfit, she recognized the demand for her product. She told friends at school and church, her stepmother spread the word on Facebook, and "soon, people were asking for bows." She learned about YEScarolina when she was twelve.

What is your typical day like, and how do you do your work?

Most of the hair bows are made on Saturday when I have more free time. First, I have to buy the supplies, decide what design/color I need, and then put the bows together. Once I get started, it doesn't take too long to complete a bow. I like to find new designs, such as puzzle pieces, balloons, etc., instead of using the traditional ribbon bows. The part that is most fun for me is coming up with the designs. I especially enjoy the creative side of the business.

In middle school, I take advanced honors classes. Also, I am in the Beta Club, run for the high school track team, and I am involved in ballet. I participate in my church, where I attend Acteens, and am a member of the Youth Choir, the Hand Bell Team, and the God Rod Team. Because I have many siblings, I also spend a lot of time attending their events and activities.

How would your best friend describe what you're doing?

My best friend has a younger sister, too, so she realizes the need for cute hair bows. She thinks it is fun to have a way of making money.

What's the hardest lesson you've learned?

There are so many things I like to do. Even during the summer months, I have camps, vacations, etc. It is difficult to set a definite time to work on bows. This experience has helped me set a schedule and stick to it.

What has been your biggest surprise?

I can actually make money! My stepmother and I worked together and made enough bows to help pay for the family's summer vacation. I know many people who make money by accepting a job, but most people my age depend on allowances. It is wonderful to be able to stay at home and make money at the same time. I will be able to drive in a few years, and my goal is to save enough money to help pay for a car.

What has been your biggest break?

I was able to attend an entrepreneur camp last summer with Mrs. Aimee Gray. She gave our group many great ideas and let us research, create, and promote our business. Also, I have family support, and they help me whenever I need it – my little sisters even help me with ideas.

What would you tell somebody else interested in business?

Be sure it is something you enjoy. Do something you find interesting, and it will be easier to fit the work into your schedule. Set goals for the future to motivate you. Be sure you have a clear plan of what you want to do and what you need to accomplish.

What do you expect to be doing five years from now?

I plan on being a freshman in college. I plan to continue being involved in my community and church and making extra money with "Out of the Box Bows." One thing I would like to do is involve some charitable organization with my business. It would be especially nice to donate bows to underprivileged little girls. Sometimes I think about being an architect or psychologist. Some of my family thinks I should be a teacher. Even if I choose a career that doesn't involve business, I can always make bows for little girls.

Hunter Dean

Biofuels Dealer

"Have the strength to learn from your mistakes and keep trying. Persistence truly makes a great businessman."

Age: 17
Community: Beaufort
Beaufort High School
Teacher: Mr. Roger Roberg

H unter Dean has found his niche in the green economy, though this young man hardly seems green when it comes to business experience. At age 17, he owns Beaufort Biofuels, L.L.C. He not only converts diesel engines to run on vegetable oil, but he has found a market for the biofuel needed, processing it and selling it to consumers.

When did you hear about YEScarolina?

I learned about YEScarolina in 2009 from taking Mr. Roberg's entrepreneurship class at Beaufort High School.

What is your typical day like, and how do you do your work?

On a typical day I collect oil from restaurants and then filter it. I store the filtered oil in 55-gallon barrels. I then fill up containers to ship to my customers. The oil must be filtered down to about 10 microns to be useable. Once the oil is filtered, I store it until it is ordered by my customers.

How would your best friend describe what you're doing?

My best friend would describe what I am doing as impressive. Some of the mechanical issues from having an engine run on vegetable oil can be difficult to deal with.

What's the hardest lesson you've learned?

Becoming a successful entrepreneur and business owner was an experience of trial and error. One cannot be simply born to be a great businessman. On the path to financial success are many failures, but have the strength to learn from your mistakes and keep trying. Persistence truly makes a great businessman.

What has been your biggest surprise?

My biggest surprise was the fact that diesel engines can run on vegetable oil.

What has been your biggest break?

My biggest break was the permit that Beaufort County issued me to pick up their oil.

What would you tell somebody else interested in business?

I would tell someone who wanted to do this that the eco-filtering process can be very messy and time-consuming.

What do you expect to be doing five years from now?

I plan to be attending college.

Elyse Delgado

Cookbook Publisher

"Think about what you really want to do and if your heart is really into it."

Age: 17
Community: Charleston
West Ashley High School
Teacher: Ms. Eva Rutiri

Cooking up a good business plan, Elyse Delgado hit upon the idea of selling a high school cookbook that would also bring in food pantry donations to help people in need. The word gets around: Soon, customers who had heard about the cookbook were approaching Elyse in the school hallways asking how to get a copy and make a contribution.

What is your typical day like, and how do you do your work?

I go to school and by 2:30 I am on the lacrosse practice field. Then I go home to do homework and relax for another day. For my business, I approach teachers and students and ask them if they would like to buy a cookbook and help a good cause, or usually I reach people by e-mail. Often people come to find me in school to make a purchase.

How would your best friend describe what you're doing?

My friends think it's awesome that I am doing this. It's so fun to tell my friends about my journey with YEScarolina and how it has helped me with my future and to meet new people.

What's the hardest lesson you've learned?

The hardest lesson so far would be how to handle school work and business work. Also, how to handle inventory, and figuring how much my cookbooks are going to cost and how much people are willing to pay.

What has been your biggest surprise?

My biggest surprise was how many people actually wanted to buy my cookbook and help out with the donations to the Food Pantry.

What has been your biggest break?

My biggest break so far was when Mr. Bailey came to me and actually wanted to help and make my idea into a reality for me.

Thank you, YEScarolina, Mr. Bailey, and my teacher Eva Rutiri. Without their help and support, I would have never been able to actually make my cookbook into a reality and help many young kids with the donations to the West Ashley Food Pantry.

What would you tell somebody else interested in business?

Think about what you really want to do and if your heart is really into it.

What do you expect to be doing five years from now?

I plan to be attending Charleston Southern University and getting my degree in sports physical therapy.

Hillman Garrett Dorn

Roof and Gutter Serviceman

"Think long and hard about the target market and how to go about marketing to the right people."

Age: 18

Community: Meriwether, Edgefield County

Strom Thurmond High School

Teacher: Ms. Jean Vess

After school is when the hard work begins for Hillman Garrett Dorn, who has made a name for himself servicing roofs and gutters in his region. To provide clients with fair estimates, he first sizes up the scope of the job, considering not just the time and materials needed but also the pitch of the roof – and how far off the ground he must work. And along the way to success, he has learned a thing or two about marketing, as well.

When did you hear about YEScarolina?

I was sixteen years old. YEScarolina has been my biggest break so far, because they helped to turn what was just an idea on paper into a reality. Without them, I would not have had the ability, or the fortitude, to run a profitable business. I would like to thank them, and Jenny Whittle, Lancie Alfonso, and my teacher, Jean Vess. Without their help and support, I would never have been able to put my plans into action.

What is your typical day like, and how do you do your work?

In a typical day, I go to school first, and afterwards, I go to the house that I am working on. Depending on the house, I may spend three to four hours working and then cleaning up. When contacted by a prospective client, I first go to their house to inspect the roof. I have put together a formula of costs, including square footage, roof incline, length of the gutters, and whether or not it's a first or second story home. I then give this bid to the client, and if they accept, I set up a date to begin servicing the roof.

I begin by setting up ladders and then securing them. Then, I rake all debris, such as pine needles, leaves, and branches, off the roof and into piles I can later take to the dump yard. Next, I clean out the gutters. Finally, I call my client to see that the work is satisfactory. If it is, I accept my payment, reschedule a new date, and pack up my ladders and bags of debris.

How would your best friend describe what you're doing?

My best friends think what I am doing is great. They benefit from my business because sometimes I employ them when jobs are too big for me to handle on my own.

What's the hardest lesson you've learned?

The hardest lesson is how to account for variable costs and to raise my prices. This was hard for me to understand at first, because when I was starting out, I had no idea that my business would be as profitable as it is now. I realized my prices were too low. What I thought was an outrageous price was actually a really good deal.

What would you tell somebody else interested in business?

I would tell them to think long and hard about the target market and how to go about marketing to the right people. Without that, you really don't have the base to even start your business, let alone allow it to grow.

What do you expect to be doing five years from now?

I plan to be well into my first year of law school.

Essence Eaddy

Day Spa Operator

"Go for your dreams, no matter how long it will take you to achieve them. Dream big and don't stop."

Age: 20

Community: Marion

Francis Marion University Biz Camp

Teacher: Ms. Brianna Zhang

M any young women like to get together to style hair and try on makeup. Essence Eaddy won't stop there: She plans to open a day spa where "you can get your nails, hair, makeup and massages done all in one place." And she dreams even bigger: not just one Essence Day Spa, but a chain of spas, with her own line of hair-care and makeup products. The customer's comfort is the key – "to make your day feel calm and relaxed." She was introduced to YEScarolina at age 17.

What is your typical day like, and how do you do your work?

I attend classes at Florence Darlington Technical College. On some days I have a dance practice, and then I attend choir practice. I also work at a hair salon. While I'm there, I do hair and nail styles.

How would your best friend describe what you're doing?

My best friend would say that it's a great idea to start working on living my dreams. She would also say that I don't give up; I always keep trying, no matter what happens. But she would say I stay calm through anything. She would say this career would be fun. You get to do hair, nails, massages and makeup all day, making people feel beautiful.

What's the hardest lesson you've learned?

Don't work under stress. If you do, you tend to get off track, so stay calm. You can do whatever you set your mind to do, and don't let people talk you down from your dreams.

What has been your biggest surprise?

I would say the biggest surprise was receiving a letter about the book and being asked to send in this bio about my experience with my business. I never would have thought that I would see my name or picture in a book for people to read about.

What has been your biggest break?

My biggest break so far is finishing cosmetology school, and working at the salon and learning more about the business of hair. However, I have learned the most from my mother, who helped me be where I am at now.

What would you tell somebody else interested in business?

Go for it. Don't let anyone stop you. If this is what you want to do and you have a passion for it, do it – because this field will take you places you never dreamed of. You can go as far as you want to go. Just believe in yourself. Go for your dreams, no matter how long it will take you to achieve them. Dream big and don't stop.

What do you expect to be doing five years from now?

I'll be working at the hair salon and looking for places to hold my spa. I'll be taking more classes in hair, nails, makeup and massage. I would also like to teach classes to students about hair.

Zakira D. Felder

Child Care Provider

"The love of being with children is a gift."

Age: 12
Community: Gresham
Francis Marion University Biz Camp
Teacher: Ms. Brianna Zhang

When your passion becomes your livelihood, you are on the path to a fulfilling career. Zakira D. Felder has a passion for taking care of children, so she started a babysitting business called "Little Thoughts, Big Dreams." When she gets older, she plans to start a day-care and eventually have one in every state in America.

What is your typical day like, and how do you do your work?

I spend most of the day in school, and whenever I get home I start my babysitting duties. I figure out who I'll be baby-sitting that weekend. I think that the love of being with children is a gift and is something so amazing that at times it is hard to explain.

How would your best friend describe what you're doing?

My best friend Rion describes what I am doing as amazing. She has even given me advice and tips on babysitting. "Zakira is passionate in everything she does and I give her props for that," she says.

What's the hardest lesson you've learned?

When I did my first babysitting job, I didn't think it would be hard to get kids to sleep when it was their bedtime. I was so wrong.

What has been your biggest surprise?

My biggest surprise was how easy babysitting is. I thought it was going to be hard, especially watching more than one child. After you start babysitting, it gets easier the longer you do it.

What has been your biggest break?

One time I had to babysit four kids who were 1, 3, and two 6-year-olds. Now that was a handful. Luckily I had help from my cousin. Time went by so fast. I expected it would be a disaster, but I was wrong.

While I was at school one day, my guidance counselor told me about the biz camp and thought it would be a good opportunity for me. I would like to thank YEScarolina for coming down into my area and introducing me to the business world. If YEScarolina had not come, I would not have known how to start my business.

What would you tell somebody else interested in business?

Think about what you really want to do and if your heart is really into it.

What do you expect to be doing five years from now?

Don't ever give up in whatever business you desire to start. Just because you might not get something right the first time doesn't mean you won't get it right the next time. Keep your eyes on the prize.

Tyler Freeman

Cornhole Game Board Maker

"You need to have the hunger to take your business to the next level and make a name for yourself."

Age: 16
Community: Isle of Palms
Wando High School
Teacher: Ms. Misty Pallotta

Tyler Freeman knows a fundamental truth for business success: Identify a trend that's likely to grow, and position yourself as a player in that market who offers the best. As the owner of Charleston Cornhole Company, he builds boards for the popular game in which teams toss bags of corn at a target. He hand-paints the boards in a choice of colors and with a customized logo, and he knows the value of Internet networking: His company has its own Facebook page with information and photographs.

When did you hear about YEScarolina?

I heard about YEScarolina from taking Ms. Pallotta's entrepreneurship class at Wando High School at age 16.

What is your typical day like, and how do you do your work?

Depending on where I am in an order, I'm either sawing and assembling the boards or painting one of the multiple coats for a smooth, even coverage. I work carefully. First I saw the wood to correct length, including sawing a hole in the plywood sheets and cutting a semicircle on the legs so they can fold in and out. Then I screw the frames together, screw the plywood sheets onto the top of the frame, and then bolt the legs on the inside. I put a coat of primer on and then two coats of outdoor semigloss paint. Then I draw on the logo and paint it and the outside stripes with two coats of outdoor paint.

How would your best friend describe what you're doing?

"If I was a piece of wood, I would want to be one thing in life: a cornhole board made by Tyler Freeman. What I'm saying is that what you do is pretty cool."

What's the hardest lesson you've learned?

Being slack with completing the orders only creates stress for me and frustration for the customer.

What has been your biggest surprise?

I can make more money having fun doing what I love to do, with a much more flexible schedule.

What has been your biggest break?

Had to be when my entrepreneurship teacher and I sent e-mails to her friends and family, bringing me numerous orders of boards.

What would you tell somebody else interested in business?

What I'd tell somebody else who wanted to do this: Use good quality wood. Cheap wood will show up in your work and will not look as good or last as long as some of the higher quality lumber.

The will and passion to become a successful entrepreneur is not something that can be taught. You need to have the hunger to take your business to the next level and make a name for yourself. Priority is key: family first, school second, business and lacrosse third.

What do you expect to be doing five years from now?

I will be attending college.

Detria L. Graham

Photographer

"Having the courage to be you, when everyone else is the same, makes a great and successful entrepreneur."

Age: 18

Community: Florence

Francis Marion University Biz Camp

Teacher: Ms. Brianna Zhang

"I love photography" is what Detria L. Graham mentions first when asked about her career path. "My mother would always buy me disposable cameras, which nurtured my passion for photography." Detria knew she wanted to start a photography business, but she had a passion for pets, too. She figured she could combine her interests in a business called Paws & Caws Photography, "the best of both worlds." She has since decided to expand: Why limit her market?

When did you hear about YEScarolina?

I was selected to attend Francis Marion University's YEScarolina's Biz Camp in 2007. I would like to thank YEScarolina for supporting my dream. I appreciate the time and effort that they invest into their students.

What is your typical day like, and how do you do your work?

I am your typical freshman at the University of South Carolina Upstate, except I receive requests for photo shoots. I am a freshman senator in Student Government Association; an events coordinator for the Marketing Association Club; a member of Impact, which is a community service organization; and Ignite, a Christian community organization. I meet with at least two organizations twice a week, and I enjoy every ounce of my time with them.

I am focused. My favorite part of my work comes when I can sit at my laptop and review the images. I love editing photos and designing images. I use a variety of photo editing programs. I help organizations design flyers to spread around the campus.

How would your best friend describe what you're doing?

My best friends would explain that I've never been without a camera by my side and that photography is in my blood. They know that my ultimate goal is to have my own studio. My friends believe I should continue my business while I'm in college.

What's the hardest lesson you've learned?

I had to understand that starting my business right now may not be the best idea because of my heavy involvement in the university. My college education is the most important job I have, and I don't have as much time as I would like to give. Also, I figured that a pet photography company limits my market; therefore, my photography business won't be just for animals.

What has been your biggest surprise?

I was quite surprised and disappointed when I learned that there was already a business named Paws and Claws Photography. Actually, there are many businesses with "paws and claws" in their name. Nevertheless, it forced me to be more creative.

What has been your biggest break?

I was selected by YEScarolina as one of the top entrepreneurial students of the year. I spent a week at College of Charleston. I also really enjoyed the other students, and everything we learned about being an entrepreneur. It was my best experience with YEScarolina yet!

What would you tell somebody else interested in business?

Be prepared to work hard, and don't be afraid to stand out among your peers. Having the courage to be you, when everyone else is the same, makes a great and successful entrepreneur. Passion is crucial when desiring to start a business as well. If you don't believe in your product or service, no one else will either. Money is a good reason to start a business, but it is not the reason one should start a business. In tough times, your passion and love for what you do will exceed all.

What do you expect to be doing five years from now?

I will be finished with my bachelor's degree and enrolled in a graduate program in the state that I plan to live in. Also, I will have started my photography business. With the right investors and enough monies set aside, I'm sure I'll be on the right track to officially and finally calling this business my very own.

Maggie Grisell

Cookie Baker

"The hardest thing I've learned so far is that you have to lose money before you will start to make it."

Age: 16

Community: Greenville

Greenville Senior High Academy of Law, Business and Finance

Teacher: Ms. Anne Marcengill

M aggie Grisell calls her cookie business "Grizookies" – "the most delectable and 'ginormous' cookies that have ever reached your mouth." It's a secret family recipe that she learned from her mother, and a legend, she says, among all who have tasted it. She has come to understand the business concept that giving out samples can dramatically increase sales. She already plans to expand. She heard about YEScarolina when she was 15.

What is your typical day like, and how do you do your work?

After school, soccer practice, and homework, I dedicate my time to cooking (cookies of course!), babysitting, or hanging out with friends. I set aside time to make sure I can fully concentrate on making the cookies. I usually do it with my mother, who originally taught me her handiwork. When they are done and correctly packaged, I play a huge role in marketing them at my school for sales.

How would your best friend describe what you're doing?

It's something that I enjoy doing, and something at which my family is very skilled.

What's the hardest lesson you've learned?

The hardest thing I've learned so far is you have to lose money before you will start to make it. Sometimes you have to give away free cookies so people accept how good they are, because people only like to buy what they know.

What has been your biggest surprise?

My cookies were able to sell at a very high price of $1.50, because the size makes up for the price. Initially, that sounds very high, but once the customer sees the cookie and tastes it, the demand is so great that they easily sell for this.

What has been your biggest break?

My biggest break was establishing a huge market at my school, where I was able to sell about thirty cookies a day simply by word of mouth.

What would you tell somebody else interested in business?

I would tell them to try it, because it's the customers that will tell you if your business will succeed or fail. If it's good enough, they'll keep coming back; if not, you know you should start over.

What do you expect to be doing five years from now?

I'll be a junior in college, hopefully attending Vanderbilt University, possibly to become a doctor missionary, but also, optimistically, already being a successful entrepreneur!

Travis Grose

Lawn Care

"I have to be ready to go to work whenever a customer needs me. Sometimes that is very hard to do when you are 12 years old!"

Age: 12
Community: North Augusta
Merriwether Middle School
Teacher: Mrs. Jean Vess

S ince he was a toddler, Travis Grose has been helping out in the yard. And now this enterprising young man is turning his willingness to work into a money-making venture.

When did you first hear about YEScarolina?

I started thinking about an idea for a business plan in Mrs. Vess' class in sixth grade. I decided to make a plan for a lawn care business because I have a lot of experience. I have helped my dad and grandparents in the yard since I was old enough to walk. My lawn care business is geared towards the elderly who can't take care of their yards and young families who are too busy to take care of their yards.

What is your typical day like, and how do you do your work?

I do anything in the yard that a customer wants me to do except hedge trimming. My dad won't let me do the hedge trimming yet because he thinks that it is too dangerous right now at my age. I will be able to add it to my list of services when I get a little older. Some other services that I do are cutting grass, blowing off or raking

THE SPIRIT OF OUTREACH

leaves, spreading mulch, picking up dog poop, and putting cedar chips in dog houses to keep them warm. I also help fertilize gardens by spreading the dog poop in them.

What's the hardest lesson you've learned?

The hardest lesson I've learned so far is that I have to be ready to go to work whenever a customer needs me. Sometimes that is very hard to do when you are 12 years old!

What has been your biggest surprise?

My biggest surprise so far is that I was asked to compete in Charleston at the Mark Motley Statewide Business Plan Competition. I was a little overwhelmed at first because everyone else there was older than me. However, I really enjoyed the competition and was very excited to go back in October to be honored at the gala for YEScarolina.

What would you tell somebody else interested in business?

I would tell other people that if you work hard and do your best, anything is possible.

What do you expect to be doing in five years from now?

In five years, I will be a senior in high school. I will be able to drive to my jobs instead of having to get my dad to take me. I will also be looking at colleges to go to and deciding on a major. Right now I am interested in learning more about business and entrepreneurship in college.

John Jenkins

Men's Jewelry and Accessory Salesman

"After I began running my business, my friends have become more interested in entrepreneurship."

Age: 17
Community: Dalzell
Crestwood High School
Teacher: Ms. Linda Avery

John Jenkins owns and operates Gentlemen's Guise, a retail business selling jewelry and accessories. "We are here," he says, "to serve the businessmen who want to add style to their suit" – watches, cufflinks and tie clips, for example, or neckties, suspenders and handkerchiefs. It's a growing market, he says, and as the lead salesman, he travels to banquets and seminars and does private shows at homes and offices.

When did you hear about YEScarolina?

I first heard about YEScarolina at the age of 16 while taking Mrs. Avery's business and entrepreneurship class at Crestwood High School, Sumter, South Carolina.

What is your typical day like, and how do you do your work?

During the day I visit different facilities, showing my products to the customers. Once at the facilities, I take out my products and place them in viewable cases. Once the customers have made their selection, I then pack up the remaining products and return home. When home, I take inventory on product sold, and personal profits.

Basically, I am both the owner and lead salesman of Gentlemen's Guise. I purchase, sell, and collect inventory on all products. All decisions in the business are made by me.

How would your best friend describe what you're doing?

After I began running my business, my friends have become more interested in entrepreneurship. They continuously ask me questions about my business, and how to perfect their own business plan.

What has been your biggest break?

My biggest break so far would have been a large purchase order towards my school gospel choir.

What would you tell somebody else interested in business?

This is a growing business and I invite all to enter into this market. It is a fun and versatile business. "Choose a job that you like and you will never have to work a day in your life." – Confucius

What do you expect to be doing five years from now?

I hope to be concluding my years in college. Hopefully, I will have already established a stable facility for my business. Now learning more business knowledge, I hope to add the techniques towards enhancing my business.

Evan Knox
Website and Graphic Design

"I think that entrepreneurship is taking a problem, turning it into an idea for a solution, and then turning that idea into a business."

Age: 16
Community: Johns Island
Charleston Collegiate School
Teacher: Mr. Hacker Burr

E van says, "The sooner that you get out there, start your business, and build connections, the better." His website and graphic design business requires daily customer interaction followed by an endless quest to learn "more code." He reads all of the top business publications to stay on top of trends and ideas.

When did you first hear about YEScarolina?

I first heard about YEScarolina Fall 2012 during my entrepreneurship class at Charleston Collegiate. I began to regularly participate in the events Spring of 2013, and I have loved being a part of the program.

What is your typical day like, and how do you do your work?

My typical work day for my website and graphic design business, in the summer or on weekends, consists of first setting the schedule for all of the tasks that I need to complete that day. Generally, I will start the day by responding to any email inquiries. After that, I usually take time to finish my current website projects. About 11 a.m., when people are likely to be in their offices, I put my projects on hold to make any follow-up calls and sales calls for the day. The rest of my day from there consists of continuous work on projects as well as miscellaneous business tasks (such as researching new content management systems, payment systems, and software to help me better manage my business). At the end of my day, I usually take up to an hour to learn more code. As a website designer, the more code that I know, the better. I already have a fairly good grip on HTML and CSS, and I am currently working on learning Javascript. Many nights, I will also take time to read a few articles in some of my favorite business magazines, such as Forbes, Entrepreneur, Inc. and Fortune.

What would you tell somebody else interested in business?

To me, entrepreneurship is about taking an idea based upon one's passion and growing that idea into a business. I suppose that entrepreneurship is also an opportunity to grow something out of nothing, in order to fill a gap in society. I think that entrepreneurship is taking a problem, turning it into an idea or a solution, and then turning that idea into a business.

What's the hardest lesson you've learned?

I'm not sure if these are really hard lessons so much as they are challenges that I did not initially anticipate, but I would say that I have to complete far more tasks on a daily basis than I ever expected. Also, in running a business, I always have something to do. I will never reach a point where I am "done" and have no task to complete. I think that this is probably true in most businesses. While this may discourage some people, it helps to keep me interested and engaged in running my business.

What has been your biggest surprise?

Since starting my business, one of the biggest surprises has been the reception to my sales calls and pitches so far. In general, potential clients are fairly willing to listen to me and look at my work. I would say that in about 80 percent of my calls, the person on the other end is willing to at least listen to what I have to say, and he or she is usually willing to look at my samples. That has definitely been a very positive surprise in running my business.

What would you tell somebody else interested in business?

The best advice that I can give to someone interested in starting a business (especially while in high school) is to go out and do it. I was very hesitant in starting my business, and I probably spent three or four months in the "planning" phase. It is certainly important to be prepared, but once you have the bare bones, then I recommend that you start. The sooner that you get out there, start your business, and build connections, the better.

Also, teenagers (and certainly some adults too) tend to be intimidated by the concept of starting a business, but in reality, you will find that starting and running your own business is much simpler and far more rewarding than you might expect. Be prepared, but don't worry too much about planning, because a lot of things won't go quite as planned. That's what makes running a business interesting.

What do you expect to be doing five years from now?

In five years, I plan to be attending college and majoring in either computer science or entrepreneurship. By that point, I hope to have grown the annuity from Bullseye Web Designs to be large enough that I can fund a software startup of my own, most likely creating SaaS [software-as-a-service] applications.

sponsored by:

Shannon Laribo
Writers' Site Webmaster

"It takes a lot of time and research to launch an idea. Don't let the momentum leave you."

Age: 16
Community: Ladson
Baker Motors Entrepreneurial Camp
College of Charleston
Teacher: Mr. Paul Smith

The power and beauty of words, from poetry to movie scripts, is Shannon Laribo's passion, and at age 16 she's clear where she wants to go with her career: Shannon intends to be a screenwriter and film director. Meanwhile, her brainchild is called Life to Pages, a soon-to-launch Internet site where writers can place their work and get information on contests and jobs.

When did you hear about YEScarolina?

I heard about it when I was 15. I applaud Mr. Tommy Baker, Mr. Jimmy Bailey and Mr. Paul Smith for being the type of people to create and teach a class of teens how to run their own business. I knew that I wanted to run my own film production company and do think I've learned that, but the greatest thing for me was coming up with Life to Pages which I never would have thought about without the entrepreneurial class that YEScarolina provided for me. I recommend all kids take a class like this because it is important to know that even when you're the poorest poor or a child bored beyond reason, you can always create an idea for a business that will bring you out of poverty or boredom.

What is your typical day like, and how do you do your work?

I go to softball practice after school most days. Right now, I'm also preparing for the Poetry Out Loud competition. On weekends, I help my parents with church affairs. And I'm constantly writing, researching about writing, and meeting established writers in all genres.

My scheduled launch date for Life to Pages is the summer of 2010. I know how I want to display my ideas and have collected pictures and contacts through networking that I can put on the website. I'm also tweaking my business plan.

What's the hardest lesson you've learned?

I've learned that it's not easy to implement an idea or to get what you want done when you want it done. It takes a lot of time and research to launch an idea.

What has been your biggest surprise?

It was a surprise for me to find that there were other websites similar to my idea for me to compare it with.

What has been your biggest break?

I'd say it's the networking I'm doing outside of the project. I now know lots of published writers and screenwriters and poets that I can contact for information about jobs and opportunities and also connect with them for a more stable and trustworthy site.

What would you tell somebody else interested in business?

Don't let the momentum leave you. Prioritize right away and figure out if you're capable of doing something like this (making your own business). Understand exactly how you want to do what you're doing, and go for it.

What do you expect to be doing five years from now?

I will be a senior at New York University. I will be beginning my career as a screenwriter and film director. Life to Pages will go national and I will have created a branch from it that concentrates on writings from students at NYU. There will then be branches from Life to Pages at all big universities.

Kristen Linscott

Candle Design Business

"To me, entrepreneurship means having the freedom to make your own decisions, accept your own failures, and, most favorably, set your own schedule."

Age: 17

Community: Mount Pleasant

Wando High School

Teacher: Mrs. Misty Rohaly

K risten has learned that you cannot plan for everything. You have to expect the unexpected and if you start out without a lot of capital, as she did, you need to be prepared to wear a lot of hats!

What is your typical day like, and how do you do your work?

I own a business called Charleston Candle Designs. An average workday for me includes making candles, updating the website and other social media profiles, and meeting with buyers for retail stores.

To me, entrepreneurship means having the freedom to make your own decisions, accept your own failures, and, most favorably, set your own schedule. Entrepreneurship is a powerful concept. Anyone who has the drive is able to work toward improving their life and being successful. The only person that entrepreneurs answer to is themselves, and if they don't work hard, their business can fail.

What's the hardest lesson you've learned?

Through starting this business, I have certainly learned a few things. I started my business without a lot of capital, and one of the hardest things has been realizing I'm responsible for everything: the planning, designing, candle making, networking, writing, and record keeping. Some of these things I enjoy doing more than others. Writing has never been a strength of mine, so when it came to writing bios, blog posts, and informational material for my website, I dreaded it. I didn't have the money to have someone do it for me, which meant I just had to push through and force myself to do it to the best of my abilities.

What has been your biggest surprise?

At the risk of sounding naive, one of the most surprising things I have discovered is that running a business is a lot of work. As I said before, I'm responsible for it all. Especially at the beginning, there is a lot of legwork that has to be done. It has been interesting to realize just how much time goes into a business.

What do you expect to be doing in five years?

In five years, I hope to be starting graduate school for a degree in international business. I plan to run my business through high school, and I hope to be able to maintain it through college. This is my plan, but another thing I have learned through starting my business is that everything doesn't always go according to plan. As I transition to college, it will be a struggle to maintain my business, but I certainly plan to try.

As my business grows, I want to be able to contribute to things that improve the Charleston community. My candles are all inspired by Charleston; the welfare of Charleston residents and the land is important to me and my business.

Joseph Long
Retail Apparel Business

"Time management is of the utmost importance. Managing and evaluating time is what can lead to the success or failure of your business."

Age: 15
Community: Anderson
Crescent High School
Teacher: Ms. Aimee Gray

All businesses require good time management skills, and Joseph's retail business is no different. He takes a philanthropic approach to profitability and has been giving money to his sister for a necessary operation.

When did you first hear about YEScarolina?

I first learned about YEScarolina when I took part in an entrepreneurship camp over the summer. We learned important business skills and how to make a profit and how to value our time.

What is your typical day like, and how do you work?

I have never felt it was a hassle to grow my business, because that growth depends on my own success or failure. Often, a regular day's work involved creating new designs, figuring prices, and learning new marketing techniques.

What's the hardest lesson you've learned?

Based on all I have learned in the entrepreneurship classes, entrepreneurship is not only creating your business, but learning how to socialize and nurture the relations that you establish with people, including your customers.

Entrepreneurship is a way to become financially independent, while creating joy for yourself and others.

Creating my business and running it has not only given me more responsibility but also has taught me many lessons. The hardest lesson I have learned is that time management is of the utmost importance. Managing and evaluating time is what can lead to the success or failure of your business.

What had been your biggest surprise?

The surprises that you uncover yourself are always the best. The biggest surprise I've come across has not been from winning competitions, but from meeting the people and creating contacts that I had not thought were possible.

What would you tell somebody else interested in business?

To those preparing to start their own business, I would advise them to have a personal interest in whatever it is they plan to do. If it's not something that you enjoy, it will most likely just be a phase. However, if you have a passion for it, the business will be much more successful.

When you have a great business, you always want to be generous, and have a way to give back to the community. For my business, I have given back by giving to my sister to help her afford her much-needed kidney transplant, which could be any time now.

Bryanna McCain
Youth Tutor

"I would tell anybody who wants to be their own boss to prepare for the worst but aim above the best."

Age: 18
Community: Edgefield County
Strom Thurmond High School
Teacher: Ms. Jean Vess

Seventeen-year-old Bryanna McCain was helping younger students with their homework when she began thinking about her church, Carey Hill Baptist, and the potential of the children there. So many want to excel in school, she knew, and she realized she could make a difference in their lives. Her pastor was enthusiastic about her business plan, offering her the use of the building and any other help he could provide as she launched her enterprise.

When did you hear about YEScarolina?

I first heard about YEScarolina while participating in Ms. Jean Vess' Marketing and Entrepreneurship classes. She has truly encouraged me to exceed in business.

What is your typical day like, and how do you do your work?

Like any other entrepreneur, my schedule is very busy. On a typical day, I finish my last class at one o'clock in the afternoon and go to work at two o'clock until six thirty. After work, I complete all paperwork and do my homework. Around ten o'clock at night, I'm preparing to end my day as a young entrepreneur.

How would your best friend describe what you're doing?

My best friend, Danielle Hamilton, has always supported me through everything I have done. She tells everyone that I'm a caring young lady that's making a difference in our economy through children. "She's showing off her uniqueness by proving that the youth can help the youth" is what my mother says.

What's the hardest lesson you've learned?

Although I enjoy what I'm doing, it has not been easy. The hardest lesson I've had to learn was time management. Managing my time has made my life so much easier. In the beginning, I never could find time to complete homework, but now, I have time to spend with my family and not feel as stressed. Anybody that wants to make a difference needs to learn the same lesson.

What would you tell somebody else interested in business?

I would tell anybody who wants to be their own boss to prepare for the worst but aim above the best.

Jesus Oljujuan Christopher McCreary

Barber

"Be patient: Some days are going to be slower than others, but it will always be worth it."

Age: 18
Community: Rock Hill
Rock Hill High School
Teacher: Ms. Jennifer Molnar

"**F**resh Cuts" is the name for a special kind of barber shop that Jesus Oljujuan Christopher McCreary envisions, as his slogan explains: "Bring a Fresh Cut to Your Life Every Time." Chris, as he's called, dreams of a spot where friends will gather and leave refreshed both in body and spirit. As he paid for a haircut once, the barber pulled out a big wad of cash – and Chris saw his future. Now, while he hones his skills (he's had apprentice training and cuts friends' hair), he's thinking through the business logistics – such as setting up an L.L.C. to protect his assets.

When did you hear about YEScarolina?

I was 18 and in Mrs. Molnar's Introduction to Business and Marketing when I first heard about YEScarolina.

What is your typical day like, and how do you do your work?

My typical day at Fresh Cuts would start by brewing a fresh pot of coffee for my customers and open up at 7 a.m. on weekdays. The TV would be on Sport Center. Customers would come in and out of Fresh Cuts seeing old friends and making new friends in my networking environment. Fresh Cuts is better than the competition because I make customers feel welcome, have a good location, and my business philosophy is customer satisfaction!

How would your best friend describe what you're doing?

My friends love what I am doing! Now that I am becoming a better barber, my friends let me cut their hair.

What's the hardest lesson you've learned?

The hardest lesson I've had to learn so far as a future business owner is that everything is not going to go the way you want it to.

What has been your biggest break?

My biggest break so far is having the opportunity to detail my business in a professional format. Another opportunity is a shot at winning the start-up money to make Fresh Cuts a reality.

What would you tell somebody else interested in business?

Be patient: Some days are going to be slower than others, but it will always be worth it.

What do you expect to be doing five years from now?

I will be expanding Fresh Cuts by delivering quality haircuts with excellent customer service. I would also like to pursue a degree in psychology.

Takisha McCullough

Graphic Designer

"Since this is a service-based business, it will always be what the consumer wants; you just have to bring their ideas to life."

Age: 18

Community: Charleston

West Ashley High School

Teacher: Ms. Eva Rutiri

The future for Takisha McCullough promises to fly high on Gracious Wings, the name of her graphic design business. She creates a variety of graphics, both animated and nonanimated, including web-page designs, banners and layouts. She also specializes in photo retouching. She heard about YEScarolina when she was 17.

What is your typical day like, and how do you do your work?

I wake up early for school, and after school I relax and then start working on graphics/designs that people have asked me to do for them. I do my homework, and at the end of the day, I talk to my friends, draw and write stories.

For Gracious Wings, I create and produce the graphics and make sure that they are working and that everything is organized. My work instruments consist of my drawing tablet and a computer mouse and Adobe Photoshop CS3, the main software program I use for all of my work. Lately, I have been doing a lot of photo retouching, filling customer requests. When I meet with the consumer, I will show them the photo and discuss anything that will need to be added or removed. I am usually paid for my services before the job.

How would your best friend describe what you're doing?

She would probably say that I'm doing what I love. She knows I love editing and how much I love using Photoshop. She's my best customer, to say the least!

What's the hardest lesson you've learned?

The hardest lesson I've learned thus far is that not everyone will like what you have done. There will be a lot of criticism and sometimes even a bit of restriction on your creativity. Since this is a service-based business, it will always be what the consumer wants; you just have to bring their ideas to life.

What has been your biggest surprise?

My biggest surprise so far was the recognition I have gotten for my work. I was in shock when I was told that my graphics were good, and that encouraged me to strive and do my best with my passion.

What has been your biggest break?

I have been asked to serve as an intern for Charlestowne Landing for my graphic design skills. Also, I was asked to create and design a webpage for Career and Technology Education with the Charleston County School System. The webpage is published, and you may see my design and animation skills online: http://www.ccsdcareeracademies.com/

Also, I have worked with a small business in Charleston with a few banners.

What would you tell somebody else interested in business?

I would tell them to work hard and play hard. If you love it, keep doing it even with all the criticism that follows. You have to remember that with criticism comes achievement. Just do what you do and love it.

What do you expect to be doing five years from now?

I see myself working as a freelance graphic designer with a bachelor's degree and running Gracious Wings on my own or with my best friend. I also can see myself in an art studio surrounded by my work and continuing doing what I love the most, graphic design.

Denisha McDuffie

Hair Salon Operator

"Be the best that you can be at what you plan to do, want to do, and will do."

Age: 17
Community: Sumter
Crestwood High School
Teacher: Ms. Linda Avery

When she was a child watching her mother and aunt style hair, Denisha McDuffie noticed that they seemed to truly enjoy the work. She, too, developed the passion and decided to follow in their footsteps. She calls her business NeNe's Hair Salon. She heard about YEScarolina when she was 16.

What is your typical day like, and how do you do your work?

I get up about 9 a.m. and I make myself some breakfast to prepare for the day ahead of me. This is running errands for my mom, or doing hair, or maybe even baby-sitting. Then after I have completed all those activities, I like to relax and watch some TV or hang out with friends. For my business, I first wait to get a call from a customer, then ask what type of style they want so I can give them the price. Then I give them a day I am available and a time.

How would your best friend describe what you're doing?

My best friend would describe what I am doing as a skilled and dedicated work performance.

What's the hardest lesson you've learned?

In this career field, it takes time, skill, motivation and dedication, and you have to be a determined yet positive-attitude person.

What has been your biggest surprise?

The biggest surprise so far is how many people get their hair done on a week to two-week basis.

What has been your biggest break?

My biggest breaks have been earning the position to work in my cousin's hair salon, and becoming a YEScarolina participant.

What would you tell somebody else interested in business?

Be the best that you can be at what you plan to do, want to do, and will do.

What do you expect to be doing five years from now?

I will be in the military reserve and in my senior year of college, where I will be majoring in criminal justice.

Mandy McGill

Custom-Made Christian T-shirts

"You have to constantly be aware of your competition, stay ahead, and always be proactive instead of reactive."

Age: 18
Community: Starr
Crescent High School
Teacher: Ms. Aimee Gray

M andy McGill has found joy by combining two passions: faith in God, and an interest in graphic design. Mandy makes custom T-shirts with Christian themes and plans to become a youth minister.

When did you first hear about YEScarolina?

I heard about YEScarolina when I was 17 in an entrepreneurship class at Crescent High School. The course was designed to provide students with the knowledge and skills leading to the development of a business plan for small-business ownership. This is where I came up with Reppin the Kingdom.

I was raised in a Church of God home my entire life, so my religion means everything to me. Basically one word defines who I am as a person and that's "Christian." I have always loved scrapbooking and designing new things in my spare time. So after a lot of debate, I finally chose what I wanted to do with my business. I decided to create a business that designed custom-made Christian T-shirts for teens and youth groups. This business was absolutely perfect for me; it took my two passions and brought me joy. It was also a plus to be making money doing what I loved. My business, Reppin the Kingdom, was born!

What is your typical day like, and describe how you do your work?

In my line of business, I work hand-in-hand with my customers. They come to me with an idea of what they want on the T-shirt. I do multiple designs based on the ideas they give me. They tell me what they like and dislike, and we work together to get the final proof of their T-shirt. I then send it off to my screen printer where they screen print the shirts for me at a faster pace than most screen printers, allowing me to acquire my merchandise and deliver them to my consumer faster. I advertise my business in local stores and on Facebook. I have sold T-shirts at local events, but where I currently sell the most T-shirts is at school.

What's the hardest lesson you've learned?

The hardest lesson I have had to learn so far was that many competitors will have the same idea. You have to constantly be aware of your competition, stay ahead, and always be proactive instead of reactive.

What has been your biggest surprise?

The biggest surprise for me so far would be how far I have come. I never would have thought, sitting in entrepreneurship class the first day, that I would be where I am now. I took my business from just a business plan to an operating business that continues to grow. Not only did I learn things about running a business, but I also made lifelong friends and met many inspiring people at YEScarolina business competitions and the YEScarolina November 2012 Gala.

What would you tell somebody else interested in business?

The first thing I would tell someone would be that you have to be driven and have perseverance. Don't give up when times get tough. Also, you have to be very social and personal. Working hand-in-hand with customers, you make multiple relationships. It's worth it to make an impression on your customers.

What do you expect to be doing five years from now?

In five years, I will be a graduate from Anderson University with a bachelor's degree both in youth ministry and graphic design. I hope to have started my own graphic design business, creating posters, banners, etc., for businesses and local churches. I will also take on the position as a youth minister at a church, teaching and counseling teens. I plan to use my experience from Reppin the Kingdom to create amazing T-shirts for my youth group that help us stand out from the rest.

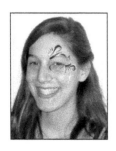

Marielle McLaurin
Face Painter

"Through YEScarolina, I have learned how to turn something that I love to do into a business and how to market it."

Age: 19
Community: Charleston
Belmont Abbey College
Teacher: Ms. Dulce Damon

Her creative flair has led Marielle McLaurin to find her business specialty: face painting. She loves designing and making jewelry, but she discovered it wasn't going to be very profitable for her because of the cost of supplies and the amount of competition. Looking for her niche, she is learning the art of face painting from a college friend. Supplies are inexpensive, and demand is high: "It's hard for parents to say no to their young child who is begging to be turned into a lion, tiger or mermaid for a mere few dollars," she says. She heard about YEScarolina when she was 15 and attended the first business camp in Charleston in 2008.

What is your typical day like, and how do you do your work?

When I come back to Charleston for the summer, I would like to be able to get a spot at the Farmer's Market in Marion Square, where my face painting will hopefully meet with success. Sports events are another great locale, as well as parks and birthday parties. While I am at school, I intend to go to local parks to paint. I will try to hand out business cards, and hopefully gain business through word-of-mouth, as well.

What's the hardest lesson you've learned?

The hardest lesson I've learned is recognizing that my first-choice business did not have a very good market. However, part of being an entrepreneur is learning how to dust off your feet and attempt something new, while making use of the knowledge you gained in your previous failure(s).

What has been your biggest surprise?

My biggest surprise so far is both how lucrative face painting can be and how difficult the techniques are!

What has been your biggest break?

My biggest break so far would be YEScarolina, for giving me the tools and knowledge I need to be an entrepreneur. As a typical artist, I would much rather enjoy my crafts than market my products; however, through YEScarolina I have learned how to turn something that I love to do into a business and how to market it.

What would you tell somebody else interested in business?

The first thing I would tell someone who wants to face paint is to get used to kids because they will be your biggest customers! Perseverance is also especially important in running a small business, and the ability to start fresh with another idea if your current plans don't work out. Finally, learn how to market yourself and be personal with your customers so that it is not simply a business transaction.

What do you expect to be doing five years from now?

I will hopefully be working on receiving a master's degree in occupational therapy. There is nothing I would love to do more than to help people for a living. As many of my patients may be children, I can treat them to a great face-painting at the end of their session!

Karen Mok

Greeting Card Writer and Designer

"My dream is to start a social entrepreneurship venture of my own, perhaps one that will promote global awareness, tolerance, and understanding among youth."

Age: 18

Community: North Charleston

Fort Dorchester High School

Teacher: Ms. Maria Williams

When poetry and design are one's passions, why not start a greeting card company? Karen Mok's business, Illuminati, emphasizes personalization. "I create each card entirely by hand," she says. "In a world that has made communication faster but also more impersonal, Illuminati offers customers a nostalgic return to times when handwritten letters conveyed thoughts and sentiments." To give back to the community, she donates all the profits from a special line of cards to a nonprofit international organization.

When did you hear about YEScarolina?

At the age of 16, I was introduced to YEScarolina. By chance, I enrolled in Fort Dorchester High School's NFTE Entrepreneurship class as a sophomore, with the guidance and continual support of my teacher Mrs. Maria Williams. I submitted my business plan to YEScarolina and was selected to attend the summer program that changed my life.

I am truly grateful to Mrs. Williams and to Jimmy Bailey and Jenny Whittle for their guidance and support. There is nothing more inspiring and uplifting than knowing that these people believe in my vision for Illuminati. Despite all the challenges I have encountered, this belief has given me the strength and motivation to pursue my dreams.

What is your typical day like, and how do you do your work?

I write the free-verse poems inside the card and design and sketch the cover art. I customize the cards so that they are exactly what the customer desires, whether this means a specific color template or an additional personal message.

As a full-time freshman student at Washington University in St. Louis, finding time to further develop and promote my business has been a challenge.

What's the hardest lesson you've learned?

The hardest lesson I've had to learn so far is how to balance what I'm required to do (school, homework, job) with what I love (entrepreneurship).

What has been your biggest surprise?

I have been most surprised by the immense support I have received from family, friends, teachers, and local community members.

What has been your biggest break?

Becoming the South Carolina Young Entrepreneur of the Year and competing in the national NFTE competition were my biggest breaks. Both of these have opened up extraordinary opportunities for me, including scholarships and networking with other young entrepreneurs across the nation.

What would you tell somebody else interested in business?

My advice is simple: Don't hold anything back. This is your chance to turn your vision or dream into a reality. Give it your all. Don't be afraid if you've never done anything like this before. You will find your experiences even more rewarding and memorable. Treasure these experiences. Stay in touch with the people you meet. Be inspired. When you look back on your experiences, you will be amazed by the person you have become.

What do you expect to be doing five years from now?

Hopefully I will be working for a social entrepreneurship organization like Ashoka. My dream, however, is to start a social entrepreneurship venture of my own, perhaps one that will promote global awareness, tolerance, and understanding among youth. Without a doubt, I will continue to think, act, and live as an entrepreneur in my future endeavors.

Looking back, I can say that my life changed when I discovered the world of entrepreneurship. The person I am today is a product of everything I have learned from YEScarolina, not only about the business world, but also about my own capabilities and passion for entrepreneurship.

Wallace Moore
Computer IT Service

"Perseverance is especially important in running a small business, as is the ability to start fresh with another idea if your current plans don't work out."

Age: 16
Community: Marion
Creek Bridge High School
Teacher: Ms. Virginia Englert

C omputers fascinate Wallace Moore and he has learned everything he can about them. He has turned that natural interest into a business perfectly suited to him.

What's your business idea?

It has given me great joy to take apart computers and put them back together, seeing how long it would take me to reassemble, later finding out how each part functions and how to run diagnostics on each part. I naturally chose what I love to do as my business.

What's your typical day, and how do you do your work?

On a day-to-day basis, my work consists of working with customers one-on-one, finding what their computer needs are, assisting them to get what they need, troubleshooting, repairing, and installing software and hardware on computers and servers. I also optimize their systems to ensure the best performance.

What's the hardest lesson you've learned?

The hardest lesson I've learned so far is recognizing that my first choice of pricing was not going to be successful. However, part of being an entrepreneur is learning how to overcome obstacles, being up for the challenge of attempting something new, and making use of the knowledge you gained in your previous failures.

What has been your biggest surprise?

My biggest surprise so far has been the unwavering support from those connected to the YEScarolina program. Mr. Jimmy Bailey, Ms. Michelle Pyle and Mrs. Jenny Englert have given me encouragement, the experience of the events and the support with my business. With this type of inspiration I have been able to continue to pursue my love for the business of computer setup, installation, repair and training.

What would you tell somebody else interested in this business?

The first thing I would tell someone who wants to work on computers is to get used to working with the public, because they will be your customers. Perseverance is especially important in running a small business, as is the ability to start fresh with another idea if your current plans don't work out. Finally, learn how to market yourself and be personal with your customers so that it is not simply a business transaction, but a relationship.

What do you expect to be doing five years from now?

In five years, I plan to have completed dual master degrees in business administration and computer science. I also plan to continue my business on a larger scale, hiring employees and expanding my service area.

Johnny Morgan Owens
Cookie Company Owner

"You never know what you can do until you try. If you put your heart and mind into something, you are bound to succeed."

Age: 13
Community: Hamer, Dillon County
Motley Rice Biz Camp
J.V. Martin Junior High School
Teacher: Ms. Laura Gasque

Johnny Morgan Owens' business enterprise is called Country Kids Cookies. "I developed what I think is the best recipe for cookies," the 13-year-old says, "and expanded it to various kinds of cookies." Running a business has been hard work, he concedes, but he has come to believe in himself. Quality control, he says, is essential – and in a cookie company, it's doubtlessly delectable, too.

When did you hear about YEScarolina?

When I was 12 years old, I was approached by my guidance counselor about participating in a summer program – the Motley Rice Entrepreneur Summer Camp.

What is your typical day like, and how do you do your work?

My typical day is promoting, operating and managing my business. I closely maintain the quality of my cookies to ensure that the reputation of my product remains good.

How would your best friend describe what you're doing?

My best friend would describe what I am doing as a great idea, but a lot of hard work. He encourages me to keep up the good job and stick with it.

What's the hardest lesson you've learned?

Running a business is hard work. It takes time, money and effort to keep a business running smoothly. Being an entrepreneur is a full-time job. I have also realized that I can do more than I originally gave myself credit for doing. I am thankful that the YEScarolina program helped me see this about myself. I take this task very seriously.

What has been your biggest break?

My biggest break so far is getting the opportunity to participate and win the entrepreneurial program.

What would you tell somebody else interested in business?

You never know what you can do until you try. If you don't believe it, just look at me. If you put your heart and mind into something, you are bound to succeed.

What do you expect to be doing five years from now?

I plan to attend the University of South Carolina, but I am unsure of my chosen major.

Jalon Percy

Business Graphic Designer

"Dare to dream, before your dreams are lost."

Age: 14

Community: Columbia

Midland Math & Business Academy

Teacher: Mr. Tyrus Goodwin

Jalon Percy is a businessman's businessman: Through his enterprise Designs by Percy, he creates business cards and fliers for merchants, as well as for others who need them for special occasions. "When I design my products," he says, "I have the customer's desires in mind." He heard about YEScarolina when he was 13.

What is your typical day like, and how do you do your work?

I wake up and say my prayers, then go to school. After school I do my homework, then work on my business, looking for new designs and ideas to make it better. When customers come to me asking for business cards or fliers, we discuss the designs that they have in mind and I make the products and print them on a laser inkjet printer. The customers will pick up the product, or I will deliver it to them.

How would your best friend describe what you're doing?

My best friend would describe my actions as very innovative and interesting. Also my best friend is my only employee, and he gives me advice on new software and products.

What's the hardest lesson you've learned?

The hardest thing I had to learn is that you can't give discounts to everybody. You give discounts to your best customers, and you give incentives to the others. The primary goal is to make a profit.

What has been your biggest surprise?

My biggest surprise was when I made my first customer their product and I received my first profit. That was the most exciting time in my life.

What has been your biggest break?

My biggest break was the time that I was chosen to compete in the YEScarolina competition and I won second place.

What would you tell somebody else interested in business?

I would tell someone to be sure it is something you enjoy doing. Dare to dream, before your dreams are lost. Doing what I do costs time and money and energy. It can be hard and challenging to be a business owner. Make sure you accomplish all your goals.

What do you expect to be doing five years from now?

I plan to attend the Gupton-Jones College of Funeral Service to become a mortician. That school is in Atlanta, Georgia. I also plan to have my design and printing company.

Clara Pilley

Non-Profit—Keys for Hope

"Our goal is to inspire others and let them know that people of any age can make a difference in their communities with a good idea and hard work."

Age: 12

Community: Charleston

East Cooper Montessori Charter School

Bank of America Biz Camp Instructors: Mrs. Catherine Marret and Mr. Darren Boulton

Entrepreneurship means giving back to Clara Pilley. Keys for Hope raises money to support their cause, Crisis Ministries. She has had to learn how to work with a limited budget and be resourceful when it comes to acquiring supplies.

When did you first hear about YEScarolina?

I first heard about YEScarolina from my mom. One day while I was at school, she went to a luncheon and heard about the YEScarolina Biz Camp and entrepreneurship program. I really wanted to participate so I could learn more about how to expand our idea, Keys for Hope. Going to the YEScarolina Biz Camp was a great opportunity, and I learned a lot about the costs of doing business, promotion, and having a good plan.

What is your typical day like, and how do you do your work?

On a typical Keys for Hope working day, my friends and I decorate and sell keys or speak to groups of kids about the project and our cause, Crisis Ministries. We raise money (so far, $43,000) by selling the keys at festivals or markets around Charleston. We also sell the keys at local shops. We have now started to involve local school and religious groups to help us make the keys so that we can raise even more money and involve more people. Many groups of kids like to get together and make keys.

We teach kids all about Keys for Hope and how to make a key, and also about homelessness and the work at Crisis Ministries. Our goal is to inspire others and let them know that people of any age can make a difference in their communities with a good idea and hard work.

What does entrepreneurship mean to you?

To me, entrepreneurship means kids or adults of any age coming up with a unique idea to help their community or world in some way, and maybe even turning that idea into a successful business.

What's the hardest lesson you've learned?

One of the hardest lessons we've learned through our business is how much time and hard work you have to put into making your business successful. You have to put a lot of thought into your idea and always shop for deals on supplies. That way, we can make the best use of the money we work hard to raise. Also, you have to promote and talk about your business every day if you want to expand it.

How would your best friend describe what you are doing?

My best friend would describe my business as creative, thoughtful and fun. Everyone feels good about themselves while helping others, too. They really like wearing their unique Key for Hope as a backpack charm, necklace or keychain. My friends love giving them to people as gifts.

What would you tell somebody interested in business?

The best advice that I can give to people interested in starting a business is that if you have a small idea, it can grow to become so big if you promote your business and keep working hard on new ideas. You also need help, so find good people for your team.

What do you expect to be doing in five years?

In five years, our business will be very successful. Our goal is to come out with new products, such as a "Keys for Hope Fund-Raising Kit." We hope to create a kit that groups of kids or adults can purchase to decorate and sell their own keys to raise money for any cause that they are passionate about. Each kit purchase will benefit Crisis Ministries, too. The kit will include supplies to make 25, 50 or 150 keys and information and tips on selling keys successfully.

We hope to involve over 5,000 kids throughout Charleston and increase awareness and support of Crisis Ministries. Selling the kits online could benefit other charities everywhere. We hope to show kids that they, too, can make a difference in their communities.

Tyler Shaw Pinckney
Graphic Design and Marketing

""The hardest lesson that I have learned is the importance of taking the approach of a customer. I learned to be reasonable and to not push a product that wasn't to their liking."

Age: 17
Community: Charleston
Fort Dorchester High School
Teacher: Mrs. Maria Williams

Tyler plans to start a graphic design and promotional company that will donate money to the American Cancer Society.

When did you first hear about YEScarolina?

I heard about YEScarolina in my business class in August of 2012, and I have learned that a typical day working on the job would require me to put forth great effort to make the business succeed. Being an entrepreneur means that you have a leadership mentality and have great ideas to make yourself a success.

What's the hardest lesson you've learned?

The hardest entrepreneurial skill is embracing the point of view of a customer. I learned that listening to a customer's wants and needs is the best way to offer a product to them. I have also learned that getting ideas from others makes it easier to design a coherent picture.

How would your best friend describe what you are doing?

If a friend were to describe my business, he would call it a good idea because I am trying to help small businesses get off the ground and make a name for themselves as they develop a brand.

What do you expect to be doing in five years?

I haven't started, but in five years I am planning to have my business operating successfully with a few employees. I plan to feed the hungry and donate money to the American Cancer Society.

Kesha Rainey
Pearl Jewelry Collection

"In today's society we place a greater emphasis on financial gains, but no joy can be found in that if you are doing something you have no desire to do."

Age: 18

Community: Charleston

Crestwood High School, Sumter

Teacher: Mrs. Linda Avery

Jewelry is Kesha Rainey's passion, and her dream is to make her business a global sensation. For now, her greatest satisfaction comes from her customers' delight with her collection.

What is your business idea?

While many have a fetish for clothing or shoes, my fetish revolves around jewelry. For me jewelry is more than just a pair of earrings, a bracelet, or matching necklace or ring. It expresses your personality, adds a twist of style to your outfit, adds a missing touch of elegance, or enables you to embrace a side of you that you have long kept concealed.

My passion for jewelry, particularly pearls, inspired me to establish Jadore Pearls. Jadore Pearls is a retail business that sells exclusively white and off-white fashion pearl earrings, bracelets, necklaces, brooches, and rings. I have multiple wholesalers that I select unique pieces from, and I create a collection for customers to purchase from. Even though I currently purchase from wholesalers, I intend to start designing my own pieces to sell through Jadore Pearls. I am aware of the vast jewelry market, but that will not deter me from my dream of making Jadore Pearls a global sensation. In fact, having such a large market gives me the greatest advantages because I am able to examine retailers that have acquired success, understand the faults of those who were unable to succeed, and partner with seasoned retailers to obtain support.

What is your typical day like, and how do you work?

My work is simple but complex when creating a collection that upholds the standards of Jadore Pearls, where "pearls truly are in rare form." When going through various wholesalers, I have to sort through thousands of products in search of pearl pieces. The process is time consuming, but seeing the final collection and having customers delighted at the unique pieces brings me the greatest satisfaction.

What's the hardest lesson you've learned?

The hardest lesson that I have learned so far is acquiring sufficient time-management skills that will enable me to not only complete my studies, but also to continue operating Jadore Pearls. At times it becomes overwhelming as I attempt to balance my studies and find time to select collections and fulfill customer orders. But after two years of operating Jadore Pearls, I have obtained the necessities to ensure I remain organized and find time to "simply breathe" so that I remain relaxed.

What has been your biggest surprise?

My biggest surprise so far has been the reception from numerous customers who enjoy each piece and continue to spread the word about my collection. The teachings I received from Mrs. Avery, having a nurturing family and community, and the support received from YEScarolina have been major contributors in such a large reception. I am truly grateful for everything they have done, and I know that with their help and the support of a growing clientele, Jadore Pearls will continue to prosper.

What would you tell somebody else interested in business?

"Do what you love." In today's society we place a greater emphasis on financial gains, but no joy can be found in that if you are doing something you have no desire to do. I love jewelry, but even more so I love allowing my own creations to unfold in my design book. Jadore Pearls is not just a project that I designed to ensure I obtained some financial reward and received a great grade. I created Jadore Pearls as an artistic outlet that allowed me to put all the visions I have allowed to simply float around in my head on paper and share them with the world.

What do you expect to be doing five years from now?

In the next five years, I hope to have obtained my bachelor's degree in international business and to begin pursuing my master's degree in business administration. In the midst of my studies, I will continue expanding the clientele of Jadore Pearls and more importantly aiding YEScarolina in any way that I can, even if it simply means encouraging other students to participate in the program. My greatest goal, though, would eventually be expanding Jadore Pearls on a global scale and in turn serving as an example for others to pursue one of their loves in life.

Ashley Lauren Sease
Fashion Designer

"My biggest break was hosting a fashion show, at the age of 15. With my own designs and my own work, I accomplished my dream."

Age: 16

Community: Irmo

Dutch Fork High School

Teacher: Ms. Norma Brown

A shley Lauren Sease's dream is to be a fashion designer, and she plans to call her business "Ashley Lauren," which has a certain ring of celebrity to it. But she wants to appeal to more than the slim and sleek: "I want to make women love their bodies again … and show that every woman can feel beautiful." She envisions several stores nationwide, and eventually international, in which friends of different sizes can shop together.

When did you hear about YEScarolina?

I heard about it when I was 16. I'd decided I wanted to start a fashion business at the ripe young age of 14. I was in love with making clothes and giving women a reason to smile again. I wanted to make women happy and excited about my clothes and the clothes on their bodies. My grandmother came up with the name for my fashion line. Immediately I knew that was it.

What is your typical day like, and how do you do your work?

Wherever I go, I get inspirations from everything. So, while I'm at school I still constantly think of more and more designs. I get inspired from anything and everything. After school and homework, I usually make more sketches or I drape fabrics on my dress forms. I constantly make more and more garments, as many as I can make. I have so many sketches that I doodle on the side of my notes at school.

Sometimes I don't even have to look for inspiration; it comes to me. I usually make a first "rough draft" of the garment, or a sketch. I then make any revisions I need to. Then, I decide what color palette I am going to use and what type of fabrics I want to use. Sometimes I have no idea what I want to use, so I browse the fabric store and make my first choices there. Then, I either drape or make a pattern to sew my garment. Then I basically put the pieces together. I sew all my garments myself. Most of the time I do personal orders, but sometimes friends or family come to me and ask me to make something, and I make them their order.

How would your best friend describe what you're doing?

My best friend would probably say something along the lines of my job is hard and very skilled. Most of my friends can't believe that I do what I do at such a young age.

What's the hardest lesson you've learned?

The hardest lesson was that I'm not super girl. I can't do it all. Even if I thought I could, the reality was that I couldn't do everything. I went into this thinking I would do this and I would do that, but then I realized that I won't be able to do everything at once.

What has been your biggest break?

My biggest break was hosting a fashion show, at the age of 15. With my own designs and my own work, I accomplished my dream. On July 31, 2008, I held a fashion show in my town. I designed and sewed 12 garments all by myself. It got me a lot of publicity and clients.

What has been your biggest surprise?

My biggest surprise would have to be the number of people that came out to see my fashion show. At first, I was just a little name, no one but friends and family knew who I was. I expected about maybe 50 to 80 people. There ended up being over 150 people who came out to see my fashion show. My fashion show, not anyone else's, but mine.

What would you tell somebody else interested in business?

Be prepared for failure. I wasn't really ready for that and I think it set me back the most. In the beginning you go into it thinking everything will come easily and fast. But I haven't always been so good at what I do. I had to work at it. I would tell them to not give up the first few times they fail. If they love what they are doing, it will help you to strive for your goals no matter what.

"If you can imagine it, you can achieve it; if you can dream it, you can become it." —William Arthur Ward

What do you expect to be doing five years from now?

I will be in New York City starting to open up stores. I will go to college, and after that I will hopefully be going public and opening stores nationwide.

Catherine Elizabeth Henrian Shows

Fashion Accessory Designer

"If an opportunity pops up, don't be afraid to take a risk."

Age: 16
Community: Summerville
Pinewood Preparatory School Biz Camp
Teacher: Ms. LaQuinta Yates

Fashion and philanthropy are the driving forces for Catherine Elizabeth Henrian Shows, who designs custom-made jewelry and recycled purses and owns Carolina Style Fashion Accessories. She designed a necklace and bracelet and donated half the profits to Children in Crisis, and she gives $10 to the Susan G. Komen Foundation for each "Ta-Ta Tote" that she sells. She heard about YEScarolina when she was 14.

What is your typical day like, and how do you do your work?

I go to school until 3pm. Then I have extracurricular activities like theater, school scholarship pageant or Powder Puff Football, followed by family time and of course homework. Education is priority number one as I have a strong desire to attend college. Currently, I am going through the confirmation process at church, so I thank God for the support of my family and friends.

I promote my jewelry as custom beadwork, but as my mother says, everything is for sale. So I create all styles of necklaces, bracelets and earrings while enjoying time in our living room with family or watching a movie. Design depends on the time of year and what unusual items I can use as accent pieces. In creating my recycled purses, I up-cycle old denim skirts and skorts into denim purses, take old wool sweaters and boil them down into new material, and buy clearance bras for my Ta-Ta Totes. All require some hand and machine work, depending on the level of detail involved in the new design.

How would your best friend describe what you're doing?

My best friend Jaime Tyo says, "It's awesome. Catie is a unique girl who is not afraid to live her dreams."

What's the hardest lesson you've learned?

Pricing. I know what my expenses are, but it is hard to put a value on my time. I really enjoy the creation process, so it is hard to equate fun with a dollar value. However, I have seen competitors' jewelry products where mine easily compares in style and quality of materials, but they have a much higher price tag. I am working on increasing the value of my self-worth as a part of the final product.

What has been your biggest surprise?

My biggest surprise was having some very successful home shows, which is part of my marketing strategy. Although I have a website and attend craft shows, the biggest seller is when ladies get together and they pick up, hold, inspect, and try on the pieces. The interaction of friends having a good time drives up sales.

What has been your biggest break?

First of all was the YEScarolina biz camp that I attended when I was 14 years old, which was sponsored by a local business and the Rotary Club. This experience introduced me to the business world as an entrepreneur and paved the way for me to compete for the NFTE 2010 Global Young Entrepreneur Award. I was selected for my green business plan to attend an awards ceremony in April 2010 in New York City. This was an awe-inspiring experience, and I met wonderfully talented youths from around the world. I truly gained confidence in who I am as an individual, and it has inspired me to give more of myself back to the community.

I would like to thank YEScarolina and Jimmy Bailey for his influence and support for students like me to succeed. Also I want to thank Mrs. Yates and my family for their loving support.

What would you tell somebody else interested in business?

I would advise others to have a plan, but if an opportunity pops up, don't be afraid to take a risk. Also if you don't enjoy what you are doing, then don't do it.

What do you expect to be doing five years from now?

After completing high school in 2013, my goal is to pursue a degree in fashion or costume design as well as to have an actual storefront for Carolina Style Fashion Accessories.

Nick Sisk

Diesel Apparel

"Be careful who you trust. Someone could seem as if they are looking out for your best interests, when in reality they are just trying to better themselves by any means necessary."

Age: 17
Community: Charleston
Wando High School
Teacher: Mrs. Misty Rohaly

Nick Sisk's ambition is to get a business degree and operate his own diesel mechanic shop. In the meantime, he has long-term goals for an apparel business, selling shirts at events throughout the Southeast.

What is your business idea?

My entire life, I have been participating and attending "diesel events," and through these experiences I realized there are currently no Diesel apparel vendors at these events. So I decided to start my own apparel company and sell at these events. My business is named "BlackStacksGear.com."

What is your typical day like, and how do you do your work?

I create a design I want printed on our shirt, send it to the printer, and they send them back to us in the boxes. We then sell the shirts at various diesel events throughout the Southeast.

What's the hardest lesson you've learned so far?

Be careful who you trust. Someone could seem as if they are looking out for your best interests, when in reality they are just trying to better themselves by any means necessary.

What has been your biggest surprise?

The number of people that want to buy something I created. It is an incredible feeling.

What would you tell somebody else interested in business?

Be prepared to learn a lot before you make your first million.

What do you expect to be doing five years from now?

I will have a four-year degree in business from Charleston Southern University and have a diesel mechanic degree. I will establish my own diesel mechanic shop that I will manage, while also operating BlackStacksGear.com.

Jerome Smalls

Handyman

"Nothing is handed to you on a silver platter. If you want something or anything in life, you'll have to work for it."

Age: 14

Community: North Charleston

Zucker Middle School Entrepreneurship Program

Teacher: Ms. Jenny Whittle

Jerome Smalls is "The Handy Kid," the name of his business. "I perform simple odd jobs for people who either cannot or do not have the time to do them themselves," he explains. He brings a professional dedication to his work and intends to study business and management in college to further his entrepreneurial pursuits. He was 13 when he got involved with YEScarolina.

What is your typical day like, and how do you do your work?

I go to school until 4:15 p.m., then come home and check my messages for any potential job opportunities. I will then schedule a day and time to take a look at or actually perform the job. Or I'll go back out to complete a job I already started. After I get a call, I first check out the type of job that needs to be done. I then give the customer an estimate. If I am actually hired, then I prepare by gathering the tools that will be needed. If I cannot do the job at that time, then I schedule a date and time to return.

How would your best friend describe what you're doing?

My best friend would probably say that what I am doing is different from most teens my age, and that it is a cool and unique way to be successful at a young age.

What's the hardest lesson you've learned?

The hardest lesson that I've learned is that nothing is handed to you on a silver platter. If you want something or anything in life, you'll have to work for it.

What has been your biggest surprise?

I was surprised by how much effort it actually takes to run a successful business. Between the money, the time, the desire, and the willpower, it really drains a person; but in the long run it is totally worth the work ethic.

What has been your biggest break?

My biggest break was when my Aunt Jackie asked me to paint the inside of a house. It was a big job and I needed my father's assistance. I made $175 on that one job.

What would you tell somebody else interested in business?

I would say to never give up. Also, that if you really want to do this, you must think it out completely. In addition to that, you need to set goals for yourself, and if you push hard enough you can achieve them. I love what I do, and doing something you love is all that matters, no matter how high the stakes.

What do you expect to be doing five years from now?

I plan to be attending college majoring in business and management.

sponsored by:

Emma-Grace Spach

Non-Profit—Keys for Hope

"We take old keys, recycle them, paint them, and decorate them with colorful embellishments. We sell them to raise money for our local homeless shelter, Crisis Ministries."

Age: 12

Community: Mount Pleasant

Cario Middle School

Bank of America Biz Camp Instructors: Mrs. Catherine Marret and Mr. Darren Boulton

Nonprofits are challenging! Emma-Grace and her friends have worked hard to raise money for the homeless shelter, but so far, they have already raised $43,000, through awareness building and by selling their Keys for Hope.

When did you first hear about YEScarolina?

I heard about YEScarolina from a friend. Her mom went to a lunch and heard wonderful things about the camp and about entrepreneurship, which to me means the ability of people of all ages to create their own business or product.

What is your typical day like, and how do you work?

My friends and I started a business called "Keys for Hope." We take old keys, recycle them, paint them, and decorate them with colorful embellishments. We sell them to raise money for our local homeless shelter, Crisis Ministries.

On a typical day working on "Keys for Hope," we would decorate and package the keys and create new ideas to help our business grow. We could also be displaying our keys at a local event.

What's the hardest lesson you've learned?

I have learned a lot of things through the process of our business growing. One of the hardest things I have learned is that it is very challenging to become a nonprofit organization. It took a lot of time and a lot of hard work. I have also learned that as your business grows, the more time you must put into it for it to be successful.

If a friend were to describe "Keys for Hope," she would call it a fun and creative way to give back to the community. Because "Keys for Hope" is a nonprofit organization, we give all of the money back to the community.

What would you tell somebody interested in business?

My advice for people who want to start a business is to find something you are passionate about and connect that into your product or service. I would also recommended that if you are creating a product, ask yourself: "Would I buy this?" That way you know if it is sellable.

What do you expect to be doing in five years?

In five years, I see "Keys for Hope" much closer to our goal of raising one million dollars for the homeless. I also see our business growing to reach more people through our new key kits that we are designing.

Mickey J. Suber Jr.

Photo Package Designer

"I live my life so that when I am gone, I will have made a difference. I hope you do the same."

Age: 18
Community: Newberry
Newberry High School
Teacher: Ms. Martha Graham

Your photographs are a record of your memories, and Mickey J. Suber Jr. wants to help you preserve them in fine form. This young entrepreneur runs a business in which clients provide him with their photos – from a special occasion, perhaps – and he creates a DVD, adding music, scene selection, and sometimes voice-over. "It's so much more than a slideshow," he says. He first heard about YEScarolina when he was 16.

What is your typical day like, and how do you do your work?

After school on weekdays, if I do not have a customer, I work on advertising my company so that I can get my name out there. On weekends I usually take a break unless there is some pressing work that needs to get done.

The customers give me a call to set up an appointment, and after we meet I put the pictures in the specific order they want. I then place the music in the background and add any captions that the client may have wanted. I then have another meeting with the client to make sure everything is done exactly as wanted, and then I put the DVDs into production.

How would your best friend describe what you're doing?

My best friend is all for what I am doing because he knows it is my dream – although he often says that he can't understand why doing all that work is my dream.

What's the hardest lesson you've learned?

The hardest lesson I had to learn was that I cannot do everything on my own. I need to delegate tasks out to others so the job can get done on time.

What has been your biggest surprise?

The biggest surprise that I have had would be that I could actually get this business up and running at such a young age. YEScarolina really helped me to realize that no matter what age I was, I could achieve my dream of becoming an entrepreneur.

What has been your biggest break?

My biggest break so far would have to be my teacher Martha Graham at Newberry High School; she was my first customer, the one who essentially gave me the chance to show that I could actually do what I was telling people I could do. I am really grateful for the opportunity she gave me. I attended the first-ever YEScarolina business camp and I found it to be really insightful and helpful with improving my business plan; if you are going to be successful, you have to have a great foundation. After the YEScarolina program, I began to take a lot of business classes and realized that it was truly what I wanted for my career.

What would you tell somebody else interested in business?

The first thing I would say to someone else who wanted to be an entrepreneur would be that you have to be dedicated and you have to be willing to do the work, because becoming successful means that at some point you had to not be successful. I want to thank everyone who has ever believed that it is possible to do the impossible. Keep on encouraging others to be great. I live my life so that when I am gone, I will have made a difference. I hope you do the same.

What do you expect to be doing five years from now?

I will have graduated from Valparaiso University, where I am a freshman with a double major in international business and marketing and a minor in Chinese. I hope to be beginning a really successful career that allows me to travel all over the world doing what I love.

Nick van der Toorn

eBay Consigner

"Business should always come first. Otherwise, your customers will become upset with the delays."

Age: 17
Community: Walhalla
Walhalla High School
Teacher: Ms. Harriette Templin

N ick van der Toorn had discovered how many people he knows are collectors and have gathered so much that they're eager to get rid of some of it – but don't know where to start. Nick knows where to start. Since he knows his way around eBay, he decided to meld his skill with the demand and start an eBay consignment service. "From the picture to the shipping, my business takes care of the entire process," he says. "Then, I take a percentage of the selling price as commission." He heard about YEScarolina when he was 16.

What is your typical day like, and how do you do your work?

After school, I get to the fun part of the day. This is where I will either be working on finding more things to sell on eBay and develop more consumer relationships, or I will be working at McDonald's.

When I do start my work, I first need to find the consumer who wants me to sell their things. To do this, I start by working for my neighbors and friends, and then expand to others through word of mouth. After I find a willing customer, I go to their home or workplace and take the product, continuing through the eBay process. Finally, I send them an invoice of the selling price and a check with their percentage.

What's the hardest lesson you've learned?

It is hard to establish a good, trusting relationship with customers when you don't already have a name for yourself. This is especially hard since my business relies on trust.

What has been your biggest surprise?

My biggest surprise so far is finding out how many people have collections of items that they are willing to sell, but don't have the time or enough knowledge to sell them.

What has been your biggest break?

My biggest break so far is establishing a good connection with my biggest customer. He has a collection of over 100,000 autographs as well as many other collectibles. I helped him to reduce the size of his huge collection and made a nice profit off of it.

What would you tell somebody else interested in business?

Make sure that you don't fall behind with getting the items on eBay and out the door. No matter what else you have to do, business should always come first. Otherwise, your customers will become upset with the delays and may start to think that you don't care about trying to sell their items.

What do you expect to be doing five years from now?

In five years, I will be in my senior year of college, getting my degree in international business. I would then like to attend graduate school for international business. In addition to my school work, I will most likely be holding down a regular job as well as maybe starting on new business ventures.

William Aidyn Trubey

Fishing Magazine Publisher

"It doesn't happen by itself. You have to really put time and effort into it or it won't work."

Age: 12

Community: Charleston

Daniel Island Rotary Biz Camp

Teacher: Mr. Morgan Dyer

A fishing magazine for children is Aidyn Trubey's dream, and he's in the design phase of fulfilling it. Stories and photographs will focus on fishing in the Low Country of South Carolina and around the world. The articles and advertisements will be age-appropriate and geared toward young readers. He even has a name for the publication: *iCanFish.net*, also the name of the website.

What is your typical day like, and how do you do your work?

I get up by 6 a.m. and get ready for school, heading out the door with my mom and brother. My younger brother and I attend the same school where my mom works. We leave school around 3:30 and head to any number of places. We could be going to baseball, soccer or football practice, or a game, or to my church youth group. While in the car or sitting on the sidelines while my brother practices, I work on ideas, design and layout for the magazine.

I keep a portfolio of ideas which includes notes, drawings, and sometimes just a phrase to remind me of an idea for future issues. The magazine is definitely a family project. We throw ideas out to each other and brainstorm. I already have a printer lined up, and my oldest brother, Andy, is in college studying art so he is helping with the cover and other art and design. My younger brother, Alex, does most of the "field work" since he is more of a fisherman than me. I do love going out on the boat, using the casting net and taking pictures. My mom does most of the typing and editing, and helps with decision-making. (She also does a recipe article.) Even my grandparents help; they take us out to local islands and fishing spots. I am even working on a Rainy Days column, since I enjoy video games and technology.

How would your best friend describe what you're doing?

Busy, busy, busy. All of my friends know how important this is to me. They know I spend a lot of time on it, too. They also can't wait to get their first copy of *iCanFish*.

What's the hardest lesson you've learned?

It doesn't happen by itself. You have to really put time and effort into it or it won't work. I wanted to have our first issue out already, but it isn't. I think it is important to be the first on the market, so I am really putting a lot of effort into it now.

What has been your biggest surprise?

I am most surprised at the amount of people who are excited for me and want to see the finished product. Even grown-ups want to be a part of it and tell me what a good idea I have.

What has been your biggest break?

I have made contact with a busy local fishing supply shop as well as working on a meeting with the marketing director for Bass Pro Shops at a store near our home. I want to thank YEScarolina, Mr. Jimmy Bailey, Ms. Morgan Dyer, and everyone who takes part each year to provide a camp like this. I have learned so much and know that this will help me in every area of my future.

What would you tell somebody else interested in business?

What I'd tell somebody else who wanted to do this: GO FOR IT! The YEScarolina Entrepreneurial Camp was a privilege. I learned so much, met new friends, and gained a lot of confidence in my future.

What do you expect to be doing five years from now?

I will be in my last year of high school, working on my magazine and making a profit that will support my family. I will also be making plans to attend college and join the military.

Victoria Turner
Photography Service

"It was great to have people that I hardly knew treat me with so much love and respect, so now I see those people as my family and I thank each and every one of them for getting me so far."

Age: 15

Community: Summerville

Summerville High School

Teacher: Mr. Jonathan Rushin

Victoria says that running your own business gives you the chance to improve your life — and your clients' lives, too. One of her challenges has been to overcome her nervousness about talking with strangers.

When did you first hear about YEScarolina?

I heard about YEScarolina in my business entrepreneurship class. Almost all the students who took the course were able to go on a field trip to Sam's Club, and Jimmy Bailey came personally to visit us and talk about the business plan competition. Afterwards, something unknown gave me the courage to go forward and enter my school's business plan competition. At Confetti Studios, I provide a photography service for events and family gatherings. Everyone deserves a memory that gives them a warm excitement every time he or she thinks about it. I would like to provide pictures that give my customers that feeling.

What is your typical day like, and how do you do your work?

Entrepreneurship to me means any individual who has an outrageous idea on how to change the world can do it. A typical day working on the business is exciting, but at the same time you can find me running around worried trying to think of ideas on how to make the business realistic.

What's the hardest lesson you've learned?

The hardest lesson I've learned throughout my business is the importance of being able to deliver my great idea to people so they could understand. I also had to get over being nervous in front of people.

How would your best friend describe what you are doing?

My best friend would probably describe my business as something energetic and fun, because I can really give my customers a great service and have a good time.

What has been your biggest surprise?

The biggest surprise I've come across is having a bunch of people go out of their way and help me. A lot of individuals from the mentorship program, from my school, and from the competition were there to push me and make me believe in myself and the business. It was great to have people that I hardly knew treat me with so much love and respect, so now I see those people as my family and I thank each and every one of them for getting me so far.

What would you tell somebody else interested in business?

My advice to people interested in starting a business is to go for it! Running a business gives you the advantage of an opportunity to change yourself and even change other people's lives, and once you do that it gives you the best feeling ever.

What do you expect to be doing in five years?

I have already decided to keep pushing forward with my Free Spirit Organization, which is the philanthropic part of my business. I go out personally to find the homeless and provide them with a before-and-after picture for free. I do that only to make them feel like they are special and people care about them. After all, everyone deserves a happy moment to cherish. That will be my way of giving back to the community. I also have other ideas, in which I would be working with children with cancer or who have a disability.

sponsored by:

Paul Hulsey

Luke Varadi

Fishing Charter Business

"Some of the profits I will receive from my new business I will donate toward the local juvenile diabetes foundation and help other children looking to get a special service dog. I will also donate some of my time to teaching children how to fish."

Age: 17
Community: Charleston
Wando High School
Teacher: Mrs. Misty Rohaly

Entrepreneurs need to recognize that their idea might not take off right away, but they need to stick with it! Failure is an inevitable component of success.

When did you first hear about YEScarolina?

I first heard about the YEScarolina program when I attended my entrepreneurship class. My teacher excited us about the chance for our businesses to be established and to possibly win some prize money.

Each day when we would come into class, my teacher would give us a lesson on different aspects of business. My teacher would then push us to be creative and develop our own businesses. I chose to run a fishing charter service in Mt. Pleasant's creeks.

My goal at Reel Fly charters is to ensure a fun, safe, and educational experience on the Charleston waters. I hope to attract tourists as well as locals who are looking to catch more fish and learn about the historic Charleston area.

We would apply the day's lesson to our plans. My teacher would then answer any questions that we might have about our business plan. After taking the entrepreneurship class and creating my own business plan, I had learned valuable information that helped me to feel confident and well prepared to start my business.

What does being an entrepreneur mean to you?

Entrepreneurship allows you to be creative and show how hardworking you can be through your dedication to your business. Entrepreneurship can also teach you many life lessons as you may fail numerous times before you are able to be successful.

How would your best friend describe what you are doing?

If my best friend could describe my business, he would say that it was unique when compared to other fishing charter businesses. This would help with my competitive edge. My best friend would also recognize how much time and hard work I have put into my business to make it successful.

What's the hardest lesson you've learned?

Working on my business plan helped me to study my financials as well as my marketing strategy. I had to carefully evaluate my financials to be sure that I was creating a profitable business. At first, the marketing was a challenging aspect for my business; however, after listening to local entrepreneurs and guest speakers at our mentorship program, I was able to master that field and get a good grasp on my marketing approach.

What would you tell somebody else interested in business?

After going through the process of creating a business, I learned many things that could help others looking to start their own businesses. One of the main things that new entrepreneurs need to learn is that you are most likely going to fail. It is critical that you do not give up. You must overcome your obstacles in order to be successful. You will also be spending a great deal of time on your new business.

What do you expect to be doing five years from now?

I understand that giving back to one's community is very important. The community has helped me immensely. I have had juvenile diabetes since I was 3 years old, and just recently I received a diabetes alert dog. These service dogs are not cheap, and therefore fund-raising was necessary. The community was able to raise over $20,000 for my service dog. With some of the profits I will receive from my new business, I will donate toward the local juvenile diabetes foundation and help other children looking to get one of these special service dogs.

Many children are interested in learning how to fish, but they just don't have someone to teach them. Therefore, I will donate some of my time to give fishing seminars and taking them out fishing. Community service is critical in one's new business.

sponsored by:

Shane Whitehead

Landscaper

"The hardest lesson that I have learned so far is to always calculate."

Age: 14
Community: Columbia
Center for Accelerated Preparation
Teacher: Ms. Robin Keyes

Living and learning have taught Shane Whitehead the fundamentals of business success. He runs a business that offers landscaping and lawn care, working with both commercial and residential properties. Critical to success, he knows, is planning a project to make the most of valuable time. He was introduced to YEScarolina when he was 13.

What is your typical day like, and how do you do your work?

A typical day on the job would be to prepare my equipment, look at my table of customers, and then go out and do my job. I would go to the customer's house. I look at my roster of customers, survey their yard to figure out what needs to be completed, and do it.

How would your best friend describe what you're doing?

My best friend would probably say that I clean, mow, take care, and make lawns look beautiful.

What's the hardest lesson you've learned?

The hardest lesson that I have learned so far is to always calculate. On one job I ran out of gas because I didn't buy enough.

What has been your biggest surprise?

My surprise so far was lawn equipment being donated to me.

What has been your biggest break?

My biggest break so far was making $1,000.

What would you tell somebody else interested in business?

I would tell someone who wanted to do this that you need to be careful with your money.

What do you expect to be doing five years from now?

In five years I will be attending The Citadel, in Charleston, South Carolina.

Marcus Williams

Author

"I'd tell other writers to be optimistic, patient, creative and philanthropic."

Age: 16
Community: Charleston
West Ashley High School
Teacher: Ms. Eva Rutiri

Poor Robbie, a book by Marcus Williams, tells the story of a boy tormented by bullying, with a lesson for all of us: Revenge is no solution. The book aims to build strong word skills and vocabulary and includes a crossword puzzle, quiz and glossary. Publishing the book is the business challenge for this young writer, who has a deep interest in journalism. *Poor Robbie*, he says, will be the first of many stories he will write.

What is your typical day like, and how do you do your work?

I go to school, then work at Chuck E. Cheese's. If I don't have to work, I usually relax, do my homework, play video games, or play basketball with some of my friends. Sometimes I even write silly short stories to complete my day.

When I wrote *Poor Robbie*, I tried to be very descriptive, humorous, and enlightening. After writing and editing the book and fixing grammatical errors until it was perfect, I created it on www.bookemon. com with illustrations (thanks to Mikey) and activities included.

How would your best friend describe what you're doing?

My best friends are very supportive, and they think that this book is a great opportunity for me in the future.

What's the hardest lesson you've learned?

The hardest lesson I've had to learn so far was realizing that it would be very hard to do this book by myself. Without the help of my teachers and my very talented illustrator, this book wouldn't be as great.

What has been your biggest surprise?

The biggest surprise was finding out the operating costs for this business. I knew it was going to cost me some money to run the business, but I didn't know it was going to cost me a lot.

What has been your biggest break?

My biggest break so far was when my teacher, Mrs. Rutiri, first saw the book. She encouraged me to do this book as a business.

What would you tell somebody else interested in business?

I'd tell other writers to be optimistic, patient, creative and philanthropic. The more optimism and patience you have, the less likely you'll have stress. The more creative you are, the better your book is going to be. The more philanthropic you are, the more you're going to make a difference in this world.

What do you expect to be doing five years from now?

In five years, I will be close to graduating from college. I will be creating more stories and books and will also continue to give back to my community. Meanwhile, I'm looking forward to the 2011 Washington Journalism and Media Conference at George Mason University. I will participate in decision-making simulations that explore creative, practical, and ethical tensions in journalism and the media. This is also a great opportunity to network with people from the *Washington Post,* the *New York Times*, CNN, NBC, etc.

Erin Willis

Reselling on Consignment

"Sometimes you have to spend money to make money. It does take time to build wealth, so don't get discouraged."

Age: 17
Community: Charleston
Wando High School
Teacher: Mrs. Misty Rohaly

Her budget couldn't support her love of shopping and nice clothing, so Erin Willis found a way to make money at the same time. She buys designer brands cheaply on eBay and resells them in consignment shops for a pretty profit.

What is your business idea?

I love shopping. And I have always had to pay for my own clothes. I am a waitress at a local restaurant, so I definitely don't have an unlimited budget when it comes to shopping. I love finding clothes at discount prices. I started using eBay to find designer brands very cheap. For instance I would buy a pair of designer jeans for five dollars (including shipping). When I received the clothes, sometimes they did not look good or did not fit. I took them to consignment shops, and found that within three weeks I would receive $27 for a pair of jeans. So I decided to start buying clothing and accessories and start consigning them.

I currently buy clothing and accessories on eBay for cheap and resell them again on eBay or to consignment shops. I am also an eBay "personal shopper" and "personal seller" where I take 22 percent of the profit.

When did you first hear about YEScarolina?

I first heard about YEScarolina when I was 16 years old. I took the entrepreneurship class at Wando High School, which led to the Motley Rice Business Competitions (2012).

What is your typical day like, and how do you do your work?

I buy and sell clothing off of eBay and then resell them to consignment shops or again on eBay. I work from my house and on my smart phone. I am always on eBay in some way. When items arrive, I wash them and press them and take them to different consignment shops. I get 50 percent of the selling price.

What's the hardest lesson you've learned?

Time management! Juggling work, school, and my business, "eBay Queen," can be a nightmare at times. But I learned that school comes first. Once I have finished my homework and studying, then I dedicate time to eBay Queen. The hardest thing is making sure all of the buyers are happy with their purchase and that it arrives in a timely manner.

What has been your biggest surprise?

My biggest surprise so far has been how much money one can actually make on eBay. I didn't realize how many people actually used eBay for a living. Depending on the week and depending on how busy I am, I dedicate between ten and thirty hours on eBay. I can only imagine how much money I could make if I dedicated forty hours every week.

What would you tell somebody else interested in business?

I have a couple of key things I would tell someone who wanted to do this. Be patient when it comes to making money. Sometimes you have to spend money to make money. For example, when I first started I spent 15 dollars buying a few things on eBay, and then I resold the clothing to a consignment shop. It takes three weeks for the consignment shop to sell an item and then give you the money. So for the first three weeks I was down 15 dollars, and then I got a check for 60 dollars from the consignment shop. It does take time to build wealth, so don't get discouraged.

What do you expect to be doing five years from now?

In five years, I hope to be out in the real world, graduated with a degree in business. I plan to open up my own business and/or building up eBay Queen to something huge! I also plan on getting my master's degree soon after I graduate from college.

M. Grace Youngblood
Jewelry Designer

"When you aim for the moon and walk diligently, you can hit the stars! Remember: Nothing is out of reach if you put your all into it."

Age: 15

Community: Columbia

Center for Accelerated Preparation

Teacher: Ms. Robin Keyes

A love for things lovely is at the heart of M. Grace Youngblood's creative passion. In her business, Jems to Jewelry, she pays attention to exquisite detail as she makes inexpensive but one-of-a-kind bracelets, necklaces and earrings, which she sells to friends, mentors and family. Her motto: "You don't have to be a star to have star-quality jewelry." Helping others feel good about themselves is her dream, and she hopes to make enough profit to help pay for college. She heard about YEScarolina when she was 13.

What is your typical day like, and how do you do your work?

A typical day for me begins with a quest for inspiration: I think about new designs I could make, bearing in mind the preferences of the market I serve. Then I determine if I have the right materials. If I don't, I look around for further inspiration or buy the additional materials. Then, I sit down with all my materials and begin crafting the particular pieces of jewelry I have already designed in my head. As I work, I leave myself open to any additional inspiration that may come.

How would your best friend describe what you're doing?

My best friend would probably say that, in starting a jewelry business, I'm being creative, "thinking outside of the box," showing initiative, accepting responsibility for my future, and using what I have learned in life to lay the foundation for my future. A lot of my friends and family members admire me for taking the initiative to start my own business and keep it going. Many have been impressed with my success, especially given how young I am.

What's the hardest lesson you've learned?

The hardest lesson I have had to learn during this entrepreneurial adventure came by trial-and-error. That was money management. Before I had my own business, I used to receive an allowance, and within a couple days my money would be gone. Now when I earn money, it goes straight into my bank account.

What has been your biggest surprise?

My biggest surprise came when I was in the eighth grade, when I was accepted into my first competition in Charleston and won first place in both divisions. What a thrill that was! YEScarolina has left me with unforgettable experience, life lessons and friends.

What has been your biggest break?

My biggest break was when my teachers, Ms. Butler and Ms. Keyes, introduced me to YEScarolina. They saw the potential in me and gave me the chance to experience my passion. YEScarolina has helped me learn a great deal about how the business world works, and it has sparked motivation in me to succeed. Over the past couple of years, I have gone to places and done things that many of my peers don't get the opportunity to see and do. Having tasted success on a small scale has only deepened my desire to become even more successful.

What would you tell somebody else interested in business?

When you aim for the moon and walk diligently, you can hit the stars! Remember: Nothing is out of reach if you put your all into it. GO FOR IT! The YesCarolina Entrepreneurial Camp was a privilege. I learned so much, met new friends, and gained a lot of confidence in my future.

What do you expect to be doing five years from now?

I see myself going to college; however, I do not see myself taking out student loans. I plan to have saved enough money by making and selling jewelry to be able to pay for college as I go. I would like to get a degree in business.

Adam Zerbst

Healthy Snack Foods

"Yes, there are times of distress, but if you love what you're doing, then you won't even realize you're working."

Age: 17

Community: Charleston

James Island Charter High School

Teacher: Mrs. Anne London

S tudying the market, Adam Zerbst noticed opportunity in snack foods that are good for you. They have been good for him, too. His business has grown, and he's headed for a career in marketing.

What is your business idea?

My idea from class was to do a snack food business. I did not want to do the old-fashioned classic baked goods, I wanted to be innovative and unique, so I settled on a healthy trail mix blend that was easy to make and tasted great too. I realized that the healthy snack food segment of the snack food production industry is, in fact, a huge market and something I could capitalize on, and … I did. I now own and operate a small healthy snack food startup named Adam's All Natural. Our flagship product is entitled Cajun Crunch, a healthy, all-natural, spicy trail mix blend. I am currently in the process of trying to apply for the Charleston Farmer's Market, in Marion Square, the Charleston City Market, and establishing a small but recognizable brand within my community.

What is your typical day like, and how do you do your work?

All of our products, for now, are produced in house and are prepared and packaged fresh. I will be looking to expand this operation to a more expansive venue, to meet growing demand, in the near future. I manage all of my business' social media platforms, marketing, and advertising myself and have an established e-commerce website for easy, online purchasing.

What's the hardest lesson you've learned?

The hardest lesson I've learned so far is that you have to be extremely motivated to get where you want and need to go, not only in business but in life as well. This has been a struggle for me because, believe it or not, I'm generally not a very motivated person. On the other hand, when I enjoy doing something, like my business, I don't feel the weight of needing to feel motivated; I just do it, and do it well.

What has been your biggest surprise?

The biggest surprise for me so far is how fast this business grew and expanded into something I would have never expected. I didn't even think this business would go beyond the classroom, much less be profitable and real, but it has.

What would you tell somebody else interested in business?

My advice for someone wanting to be an entrepreneur is that, number one, it's not as hard as it looks or sounds. Yes, there are times of distress, but if you love what you're doing, then you won't even realize you're working. My second piece of advice is to network like crazy. No matter your age, people are generally willing to help and share amazing information that you'll use throughout your business and personal ventures. Stick with the old saying, "It's not what you know, it's who you know." and you'll be just fine.

What do you expect to be doing five years from now?

In five years, I see myself getting out of college and starting a successful career as the owner of a marketing firm. Moving out of Charleston and into a bigger city, such as New York, is a very likely possibility. Moving would allow more opportunity for networking and greater exposure for my firm.

sponsored by:

YEScarolina Board of Directors

TOMMY BAKER–BOARD CHAIR
Baker Motor Company

JAMES J. BAILEY
Bailey & Associates, Inc.

ERIC BOWMAN
SPARC

NATE DAPORE
PeopleMatter

KATHLEEN KEENER ELSNER
Law Offices of Kathleen Keener Elsner

WILLIAM A. HALL
Hall's Chophouse

ART HARTUNG
Art Hartung Investment Counselor

PAUL HULSEY
Hulsey Litigation Group

CAROLYN JAMES
Motley Rice LLC

MARGIE A. PIZARRO
The Pizarro Law Firm

ANGEL POSTELL
Home Team Public Relations

MICHAEL B. SHULER JR.
King Street Commercial, LLC

JAMES P. SMITH
Atlantic Coast Advisory Group

BERNARD STEINBERG
Charleston Steel & Metal Co.

APRIL STONE
Heritage Trust Federal Credit Union

AUSTIN STONE
S & S Development, LLC

JUSTIN VANBOGART
Chuck Ventures

RONDALD WHEET
Revolutions Medical Corporation

ADAM WITTY
Advantage Media Group

KATHRYN YOUNGMAN
BB&T Wealth

Youth Entrepreneurship South Carolina, YEScarolina, is the only organization in the state of South Carolina dedicated to teaching youth the principles of entrepreneurship and free enterprise. Recognizing that South Carolina's future is dependent upon a vibrant Entrepreneurial Economy, YEScarolina is preparing today's youth to be tomorrow's business owners and business leaders.

YEScarolina has helped thousands of young people from communities statewide build business skills and unlock their entrepreneurial creativity. To date, YEScarolina trained and certified over 700 South Carolina teachers on the subject of entrepreneurship. These educators in turn have touched and inspired thousands of young South Carolinians with a thirst for entrepreneurship. YEScarolina now offers entrepreneurship training to public school teachers statewide without charge.

YEScarolina is a program partner of the Network For Teaching Entrepreneurship (NFTE).

YEScarolina is a 501(c)(3) non-profit. Proceeds from the sale of this book benefit YEScarolina. Your tax deductible donations can be sent to the address below. Your help is appreciated.

YEScarolina
PO Box 210
Charleston, SC 29402

www.yescarolina.com

Why have a custom version of
The Spirit of Outreach?

- Build personal bonds with customers, prospects, employees, donors, and key constituencies

- Develop a long-lasting reminder of your event, milestone, or celebration

- Provide a keepsake that inspires change in behavior and change in lives

- Deliver the ultimate "thank you" gift that remains on coffee tables and bookshelves

- Generate the "wow" factor

Books are thoughtful gifts that provide a genuine sentiment that other promotional items cannot express. They promote employee discussions and interaction, reinforce an event's meaning or location, and they make a lasting impression. Use your book to say "Thank You" and show people that you care.

www.ingramcontent.com/pod-product-compliance
Lightning Source LLC
Jackson TN
JSHW011938131224
75386JS00041B/1443